"This beautiful little book is a perfect guide for anyone who wants an introduction to Augustine's spiritual wisdom. Clearly and accessibly written, *Praise Without Ceasing* is a treasure trove of Augustine's deepest insights about journeying home to God, laid bare for the current age."

—Veronica Roberts Ogle, Assistant Professor of Political and Social Thought and the Augustinian Catholic Intellectual Tradition, Villanova University

"James Lee's *Praise Without Ceasing* offers an accessible and insightful guide to understanding the caritative spirituality of Augustine's thought. Lee's presentation of Augustine's insight into the deepest longings of the human heart has much to teach all who are interested in Augustine's thought. Readers will benefit from journeying alongside Augustine and Lee!"

—Colleen E. Mitchell, Associate Director of Outreach, Augustinian Institute, Villanova University

"A common barrier to St. Augustine's thought is its immensity. There are so many insights that one does not know where to start and, if one does start with one element and focuses on it, such as Augustine's interiority, one risks losing sight of other elements, such as his emphasis on community. Lee's book answers this problem by being a concise, accessible overview of various elements in Augustine's spirituality with many quotes from Augustine himself."

—Austin Murphy, OSB, St. Procopius Abbey

"In this informative, delightful, and captivating book, James Lee invites us on a spiritual journey with Saint Augustine of Hippo. Its destination is nothing less than God, who is great and exceedingly worthy of praise. I highly recommend reading this book to go with Saint Augustine to God."

—Andrew Hofer, OP, editor of *The Cambridge Companion to Augustine's Sermons*

"This little gem of a book not only offers the best, concise account available of the spiritual life according to St. Augustine, it also offers an introduction to the spiritual life itself, in contrast to the series of self-help books and websites to which it is often reduced. The spiritual life is here revealed as both personal and ecclesial, biblical and sacramental, a bracing life in the Spirit in which the discipline of prayer and the ubiquity of grace are intimately intertwined, a training of the heart whose thirst for God can never be satisfied by any other path. An accessible book anchored in sound scholarly judgment and seasoned pedagogical experience. Highly recommended."

—John C. Cavadini, McGrath-Cavadini Director, McGrath Institute for Church Life, University of Notre Dame

Praise Without Ceasing

Praise Without Ceasing

The Spirituality of St. Augustine

James K. Lee

CASCADE *Books* • Eugene, Oregon

PRAISE WITHOUT CEASING
The Spirituality of St. Augustine

Cascade Books
An Imprint of Wipf and Stock Publishers
199 W. 8th Ave., Suite 3
Eugene, OR 97401

www.wipfandstock.com

PAPERBACK ISBN: 978-1-7252-6188-4
HARDCOVER ISBN: 978-1-7252-6187-7
EBOOK ISBN: 978-1-7252-6189-1

Cataloguing-in-Publication data:

Names: Lee, James K., author.

Title: Praise without ceasing : the spirituality of St. Augustine / James K. Lee.

Description: Eugene, OR : Cascade Books, 2026 | Includes bibliographical references and index.

Identifiers: ISBN 978-1-7252-6188-4 (paperback) | ISBN 978-1-7252-6187-7 (hardcover) | ISBN 978-1-7252-6189-1 (ebook)

Subjects: LCSH: Augustine, of Hippo, Saint, 354-430—Criticism and interpretation. | Church history—Primitive and early church, ca. 30–600. | Spirituality—Christianity. | Spiritual life—Christianity.

Classification: BR65.A9 .L44 2026 (print) | BR65.A9 (ebook)

Contents

Acknowledgments

I WOULD LIKE TO thank my friends and colleagues who have offered steadfast support to bring this book to its completion. First and foremost, I am grateful as ever to John C. Cavadini, professor of theology at the University of Notre Dame and McGrath-Cavadini Director of the McGrath Institute for Church Life, who introduced me to the genius of St. Augustine. Many friends from Notre Dame have helped shape my thinking, including Brian Daley, SJ; Abbot Austin Murphy, OSB; Andrew Hofer, OP; Cyril O'Regan; Joseph Wawrykow; Gary Anderson; Ann Astell; Michael Heintz; Khaled Anatolios; Katie Cavadini; Anthony Pagliarini; John Sehorn; and many others. My colleagues at SMU have offered a wealth of support and encouragement, including Bruce Marshall, Denise DuPont, Matthew Wilson, Ben Voth, Roy Heller, Pamela Hogan, Hugo Magallanes, Craig Hill, Fred Aquino, Matthew Esquivel, David Willhite, and more. I am grateful to have received a Scholarly Outreach Award from the Perkins School of Theology at SMU that helped support the research for this book. Thanks to Michael Thomson for seeking to bring this work to publication.

My wife, Anna, is a source of unwavering love and faithfulness. Thank you, I love you. To my daughters, Mary Margaret and Josephine, you are gifts from God, I love you. Many thanks to my family and friends, including Edward Lee, Young Lee, Sang Gun Lee, Hugh and Terry Burnstad, Raja and Mara Mumuni, Karl and Nora Sussan, the Cavadini family, the Arnold family, the Slonkosky family, and many others.

Acknowledgments

This book is dedicated to my daughter Josephine Chantal Lee, born January 5, 2022, with love and thanksgiving.

Abbreviations

FC	The Fathers of the Church. Edited by R. J. Deferrari. Washington, DC: Catholic University of America Press, 1947–
WSA	The Works of Saint Augustine: A Translation for the 21st Century. Edited by John E. Rotelle. New York: New City, 1990–

Introduction

The Spirituality of St. Augustine

Hold fast to the love of God, so that just as God is eternal, you may also abide in eternity; for you are what you love.
—Augustine, *Homilies on the First Epistle of John* 2.14

Over fifteen centuries ago, a humble pastor lay dying in his bed after falling ill with a fever. As he prepared for death, the world around him seemed to be crumbling. The eternal city of Rome, once considered the invincible capital of the empire, had been sacked by barbarians. His own city of Hippo in North Africa was under siege by vandals. The church and society were rife with conflict and division. Yet he continued to preach a message of hope to the members of his congregation, exhorting them to lift their hearts to the kingdom of God instead of placing their hopes in the kingdoms of this world. As his bodily health deteriorated, he requested to have the penitential psalms posted on his bedroom walls so that he could pray them constantly. In the midst of his sickness, he never ceased to give praise and thanksgiving to God. During his final days, he asked to be left in solitude so that he could offer proper and worthy penance for his sins.[1] Coming to the end of his earthly journey, he entrusted himself and his church to God's mercy.

1. Possidius, *Life of St. Augustine* 31.

His name was Augustine. The world has never seen another man like him. More than any other Christian author, he left an indelible imprint upon Western civilization. For without Augustine, Western civilization as we know it would not exist. Augustine was not only an influential pastor, theologian, and spiritual leader, but he was also an outspoken public figure and a brilliant scholar who helped shape the Western intellectual tradition. His surviving works total more than five million words and include over 1,700 treatises, letters, commentaries, and sermons. His ideas have been formative in fields such as philosophy, theology, history, psychology, politics, ethics, linguistics, education, and even physics.[2] To this day, thousands of scholarly and popular publications in different languages are devoted to the life and teachings of Augustine, the North African Catholic bishop of Hippo, who died in the fifth century.[3]

Why has Augustine remained relevant in every age and with each successive generation? Why have his works been copied, consulted, and studied for centuries? Among the reasons for Augustine's enduring influence is his profound understanding of human nature. Augustine delivers an illuminating vision of what it means to be human, and he offers practical solutions to some of the greatest challenges that we face in our human condition.

One of the primary problems that we encounter as human beings is how to become truly happy. Happiness, in this sense, is not to be confused with passing contentment or temporary pleasure. Rather, true happiness is the fulfillment of the deepest desire of the human heart, a kind of peace that surpasses the satisfaction of fleeting wants. According to Augustine, we experience the desire for happiness as a restlessness of heart. For the happiness that we seek lies beyond perfect attainment in our present condition. Only eternity can satisfy the longing of the heart.[4] Augustine

2. According to the physicist and Nobel laureate Steven Weinberg, in the field of quantum cosmology, it has become a tradition to cite Augustine's view of time in bk. 11 of *The Confessions* ("Cosmological Constant Problem," 15n13).

3. Topping, *St Augustine*, 3.

4. Le Fébure du Bus, *Desire and Unity*, 70.

learned by experience that no material thing can fulfill our deepest desire. We are spiritual creatures in search of a transcendent end. The problem of human happiness is a spiritual one. Our restless heart is evidence that we are on a spiritual journey toward a transcendent destiny.[5]

What is the end of our journey? Augustine powerfully argued that our ultimate destination and the true source of our happiness is God. For God alone is our first cause and our final end. God is the transcendent truth, beauty, and goodness for which we long. Only by loving God with our whole being can we come to satisfy our deepest desire. Further, if we learn how to love God, then we can learn how to love ourselves and our neighbors as creatures made in God's image. And by loving God and neighbor in community, we can discover the true meaning and purpose of our existence as human beings, namely, to cling to God as one body united in love.

Given this vision of our spiritual journey, another problem arises. How can we come to know and love God? How can we arrive at our destination if the object of our happiness is Spirit, for as the Christian Scriptures proclaim, God is Spirit (John 4:4)? How can we measure progress on our spiritual journey? Augustine's answers to these questions demonstrate his enduring legacy and lasting impact. His thought continues to resonate with people throughout history, and it remains a rich reservoir of wisdom and guidance for those seeking to grow in the spiritual life.

This book aims to show how Augustine remains a spiritual master who continues to speak to us today. It offers a blueprint of Christian spirituality based upon Augustine's teachings, which can be applied and practiced by individuals and communities in any age. According to Augustine, God provides the way to our heavenly homeland precisely by means of Christ, the church, and the sacraments. The journey home is beset with hardship and suffering. It is easy to lose the way. Yet thanks to the merciful love of God given to us in Christ and the church, we can find our way home.

5. Martin, *Our Restless Heart*, 25–27.

The following chapters chart a course for those seeking the way to true and lasting happiness while on our spiritual journey. In Augustine's view, we learn how to love God by becoming members of the church. As part of a community bound in charity, we can begin to give praise and thanksgiving to God. We are not on the journey alone. If we open our minds and hearts to the love and mercy of God, we can arrive at that final destination, our heavenly homeland, where together with all of the saints and angels we will rejoice for eternity and live lives of praise without ceasing.

AUGUSTINE'S JOURNEY

Who is Augustine? Despite having lived many centuries ago, Augustine's life continues to be a source of inspiration for us as wayfarers on our journey. The sixteenth-century Spanish mystic Teresa of Avila once remarked that as she began to read Augustine's spiritual autobiography, *The Confessions*, she saw herself in it.[6] Augustine's story is the story of humanity, for it is about how we have all turned away from God, yet God has not abandoned us. Instead, God offers us grace so that we might find our way home.

Augustine was born on November 13, 354, in Thagaste, North Africa. He was raised by a Catholic mother of local Berber or Punic origin named Monica and a pagan Roman administrator of the middle-class named Patricius. Augustine was raised among Roman citizens in North Africa who spoke Latin. As an infant, he was taken to the church for initiation and was enrolled in the catechumenate, but he was not baptized.[7] Augustine had a brother and perhaps two sisters, but little is known about them.[8] As a young man, Augustine received a classical education in Latin grammar and rhetoric. With the support of a wealthy patron, Augustine continued his studies in Carthage, one of the largest and most important cities in Roman North Africa.

6. Teresa of Avila, *Book of Her Life* 9.8.
7. Levering, *Theology of Augustine*, xv.
8. Chadwick, *Augustine of Hippo*, 5.

Augustine described his time in Carthage as one of restlessness and longing, punctuated by the desire to love and to be loved.[9] Like many men of his age and social standing, Augustine took a mistress or common-law wife, with whom he had a son named Adeodatus.[10] During this time, Augustine also underwent a spiritual odyssey of sorts due to the influence of a group known as the Manicheans. Following the teachings of a third-century Persian named Mani, the Manicheans espoused a dualistic philosophy. According to the Manicheans, the problems that we encounter as human beings can be attributed to an eternal conflict between the opposing forces of light and darkness, good and evil, spirit and matter.[11] As spiritual beings, we seek to be liberated from our material bodies. Manichean dualism helped Augustine understand his experience of the constant struggle between the spirit and the flesh. It provided Augustine with an explanation for his restlessness.

However, as he continued his intellectual and spiritual journey, Augustine became disillusioned with Manicheism, especially after having met a Manichean teacher named Faustus who failed to answer his questions adequately. Having become a successful rhetorician, Augustine took a teaching position in Rome and later in Milan. It was in Milan that Augustine encountered the Catholic bishop Ambrose, who began to instruct him in Platonic philosophy and biblical theology. This education opened Augustine's eyes to the truth of Christianity and the falsehood of Manicheism. On one hand, Platonic philosophy gave Augustine a new perspective on the nature of evil and the relationship between spirit and matter. On the other hand, Augustine came to appreciate the Christian Scriptures, especially the narratives in Genesis, which he had previously considered too primitive. According to Christian biblical

9. Augustine, *Confessions* 3.1.1.

10. Chadwick, *Augustine of Hippo*, 11.

11. In the Manichean worldview, matter is the problem, for matter weighs down and captures spirit. According to Mani's cosmology, fragments of the divine light were captured by the evil powers of darkness and became imprisoned in the bodies of human beings and animals (Chadwick, *Augustine of Hippo*, 13).

teaching, God creates everything good. Matter is not the problem, nor is it inherently evil. Instead, evil is a privation or defect of goodness. Furthermore, Christianity teaches that God chose to become human, body and soul—a central mystery known as the incarnation. With this renewed understanding of Christian theology, Augustine finally left behind the false teachings of Manicheism.

If matter is not the problem, then what is at the root of our misery and unhappiness? On this point, Augustine turned to the story of Adam and Eve in the book of Genesis. Despite having been created in paradise and having received many gifts, Adam and Eve chose to disobey God, as symbolized by their decision to eat from a forbidden tree in the garden of Eden and to hide from God in the shadows.[12] Because of the disobedience of the first parents, death and corruption were introduced into the world. The original communion between God and creation was lost. As a result, creation is in a state of decay and destruction. The world as we know it is marked by sin and disorder. The effects of sin are manifested in the broken relationships between creator and creatures, and in the discord among human beings.

According to Augustine, the root of all sin is pride, or *superbia* in Latin.[13] Pride, in this sense, is not to be confused with an appreciation for one's gifts, abilities, or existence. Instead, it is something far more sinister. Pride is the desire to take the place of God. When Adam and Eve chose to disobey God, they rejected God's goodness and sought to become the arbiters of good and evil. Their disobedience signified humanity's attempt to elevate itself over and against God. *Superbia* is to look to oneself as the supreme power rather than God. As such, it is an illusion, for we are finite creatures who depend upon God for our existence. While *superbia* is not necessarily a conscious desire, pride is experienced in our fallen condition as the formatting of all of our affections toward the pursuit of self-benefit, at all costs. Among fallen human beings, pride takes the form of a disordered love of self over God, and as such, it is a misguided form of self-love. In Augustine's view,

12. Augustine, *Confessions* 2.6.14.

13. Cavadini, *Visioning Augustine*, 66.

this disordered self-love can lead only to destruction and ruin. Since God alone is the source of being, truth, and goodness, to set oneself over against God inevitably leads to corruption, decay, and unhappiness. Pride is a spiritual problem that leads to the disintegration of the human being, body and soul.

Now that we find ourselves in this broken condition, how can we find healing and restoration? As Augustine learned from studying Christianity, the only way to heal our pride is by the grace of God made available to us in Christ, whose humility is a healing balm for the tumor of pride. Christ, the eternal Word and the Son of God, chose to become a human being in order to bring healing to our human nature, body and soul, and to give us a share in his divine life. Since Christ is the one mediator between God and humanity, we can be restored to right relationships with God and others. By God's grace, we can undergo transformation and conformation to Christ, and we are incorporated into the one body of Christ, the church. This transformation takes place precisely by participating in the church's sacraments, such as baptism and the Eucharist, and by being part of a community united in love and offering works of mercy. The church is a community bound by charity, and our healing takes place in and through the communal life of the church.

Augustine concluded that the solution to the problem of evil is not to seek liberation from the material world, but rather to be transformed by charity, or *caritas* in Latin. Charity means the love of God, ourselves, and our neighbors, in the proper order. Charity heals the disordered love of self that is characteristic of pride or *superbia*. True charity reorders our desires so that we can love God above all things. Then, we can love ourselves and our neighbors for God's sake, that is, with God as the source of our true and lasting happiness. We remain on a journey to God as our shared end and final destination, for heaven is an eternal participation in the life-giving love of God. We make progress on our journey to our heavenly homeland by participating in the life of the church and by growing in charity. For Augustine, our spiritual journey is always communal, for we come to know and love God in the community of the church.

In the year 387, Augustine decided to become a member of the Catholic Church and was baptized by his mentor, Ambrose. After his baptism, Augustine went on a spiritual retreat with some friends in Italy. His earliest extant works were composed during this time. They reveal his familiarity with Neoplatonic philosophers, especially Plotinus (205–70 CE). Augustine also began to study the Bible intensely, particularly the writings of Paul. This had a profound impact on his thought. Augustine began to unpack the significance of the incarnation. Through the incarnation, God works to heal human nature and to provide a share in divine life by the gift of grace. Far from discarding the material world, the incarnation reveals that God redeems the fallen world so that human beings, as spiritual creatures with material bodies, can participate in God's eternal life of love. In practical terms, Augustine began to emphasize the importance of sharing in the church's sacraments. God's grace is mediated by means of the sacraments, especially baptism and the Eucharist. As spiritual creatures, human beings undergo transformation by growing in charity, precisely through sharing in the life of the church.

Around the year 390, Augustine returned to North Africa with the intention of founding a monastic community, but he found himself thrust into pastoral ministry. He was ordained a priest in 391, and then in 395, he was made coadjutor bishop of Hippo. He spent the rest of his life teaching and preaching, celebrating the sacraments, and resolving disputes, both ecclesial and civic in nature. While engaged in full-time ministry, he was an incredibly prolific scholar and author, such that his secretary Possidius claimed that it would be impossible for anyone to read all of Augustine's works.[14] Augustine left behind biblical commentaries, letters, sermons, and treatises, as well as polemical writings against groups such as the Manicheans, Arians, Donatists, Pelagians, and pagans. His teachings helped shape Western Christian thought in definitive fashion.

14. Possidius, *Life of St. Augustine* 18.

Augustine lived during a time marked by division, upheaval, and transition. He witnessed firsthand the transformation of the West from an ancient pagan civilization to a predominantly Christian society under the constant threat of dissolution. In the year 410, the fall of Rome to Gothic invaders prompted Augustine to write his lengthy work *The City of God*, a critique of the pagan empire and a positive construction of Christian doctrine and worship. Twenty years later, Augustine witnessed the siege of North Africa by barbarian invaders. Amid great uncertainty, Augustine continued to preach the good news of Christ's salvific work as the source of the church's hope. Augustine died on August 28, 430, at the age of seventy-six. The city of Hippo fell to the Vandals less than one year later. The Western world entered a period of instability, yet Augustine's influence continues to endure to the present day.

AUGUSTINIAN SPIRITUALITY FOR TODAY

Among Augustine's most important and lasting contributions is his spirituality, which emerges not only from his biblical teaching but also from his vision of practical life in the church. What, precisely, is spirituality? In the social sciences, spirituality can be defined as belief in a higher power that enables one to understand the meaning of human experience. Spirituality in this sense is universal to human beings, for all cultures have a concept of "an ultimate, transcendent, sacred, and divine force."[15] Among those who identify as Christian, spirituality can be a vague concept. Christian Smith has described the spiritual lives of young adults in the United States in the twenty-first century as "moralistic therapeutic deism," wherein God or a divine force is distant and uninvolved in one's life, and the central goal is to feel good about oneself.[16] In recent times, it has become increasingly common for people to describe themselves as being "spiritual but not religious,"[17] yet it is not always

15. Mattis, "Spirituality," 601.

16. C. Smith, *Souls in Transition*, 154.

17. Bullivant, *Nonverts*, 67–69.

clear what being "spiritual" means. For some, being "spiritual" can mean holding beliefs or engaging in ritual practices beyond the confines of organized religion.[18] Spirituality in this sense may indicate a growing alienation from the institutional church in favor of an individualistic, self-constructed worldview.

Augustine can be an immensely helpful resource in our current context. Like many in the modern world, Augustine experienced alienation from the institutional church. Yet he returned to the faith of his mother, Monica. Augustine's spiritual odyssey led him to participate in the visible church, a community united in charity by the celebration of the sacraments and offering works of mercy. For Augustine, spirituality is not reducible to an individual, isolated endeavor. Spirituality is not lived in a vacuum or in an armchair. Rather, Augustine's spirituality inevitably leads beyond oneself to union with God and with other members of the body of Christ, the church. Our spiritual journey requires turning inward to the desires of the heart,[19] yet this movement continues upward and outward with the twofold love of God and neighbor. The end of all spirituality, in an Augustinian sense, is *caritas*, the love of God, self, and neighbor. We learn how to love properly by being initiated into the church, which incorporates us into the mystical body of Christ and enables us to receive God's grace by means of the sacraments. By participating in the church's communal life, we undergo a process of growth and transformation in charity, and this enables us to make progress on our spiritual journey. An Augustinian spirituality is always communal, for we undergo healing by being incorporated into the communal body of Christ, which is the church.

Augustine also provides clarity with regard to the meaning of the word "spirit," or *spiritus* in Latin. Before having been baptized in the church, Augustine struggled to conceptualize spirit due to the influence of the Manicheans. In the Manichean view, spirit and matter are constantly at war, and in some way, spirit is limited by

18. Fuller, *Spiritual, but Not Religious*, 8–11.

19. Babcock, "Spirituality of Desire," 187.

matter.[20] However, after Augustine had read the books of the Neoplatonists and studied the Christian Scriptures, his mind was freed from the materialistic views of the Manicheans. He began to understand that God is unique as a transcendent Spirit, for God alone is "everywhere in your whole being."[21] God is infinite, immutable, and unchangeable, just as truth is unchanging,[22] for God is being itself. Yet this does not mean that God is distant from creation. On the contrary, since God transcends all material things, God is present to all things, unlike any creature. God is the source of all that exists. Finite creatures participate in God's being, whether such creatures are spiritual or material. In Augustine's view, human beings are distinct since they are created with spiritual souls and material bodies. The human soul receives life from God, and it is the animating principle of the material body. Matter is not intrinsically evil, as the Manicheans wrongly suggested, for all things are created good. Yet the spiritual soul remains unique insofar as it is capable of knowledge and love, which are spiritual activities that correspond to the intellect and the will. To be a spiritual creature, therefore, means to participate in God's being and to receive life from God. God is infinite Spirit, yet spiritual creatures are made in God's image insofar as we are able to know and love God and others. We are made as spiritual and material creatures so that we can make progress on our journey to our heavenly homeland.

Augustine offers a hopeful vision of spiritual growth and transformation. For Augustine, spirituality is a transformative encounter with the personal, triune God, whereby the intellect and the will are perfected in knowledge and love. This is a gradual process that begins in this life and is perfected only after death. The human being undergoes a spiritual journey or ascent to God, which takes place not merely by an increase in knowledge but above all by a transformation and conformation to Christ in love.

20. Mani taught that the divine spirit had become imprisoned by matter, which can lead to a materialistic view of the divine (Chadwick, *Augustine of Hippo*, 13).

21. Augustine, *Confessions* 1.3.3.

22. Augustine, *Answer to Secundus* 8.

In Augustine's spirituality, this transformation is individual, communal, and social, for one grows in charity by being a member of the body of Christ. Christian spirituality requires concrete, practical actions, such as participation in the sacraments, prayer, and works of mercy toward one's neighbors. The net effect of the spiritual life as conceived by Augustine is the healing and reordering of our disordered affections, such that we learn how to love God, ourselves, and our neighbors for God's sake. This transformation in true charity is made possible by the gifts and graces of the Holy Spirit, who gives life to the one body of Christ, the church.

Augustine's rich understanding of spirituality remains relevant today. As a spiritual master, Augustine teaches us how to direct our deepest desires for happiness and truth toward the God in whom we find rest. Whether religious or nonreligious, all human beings experience the limitations that come from being finite creatures. We are not entirely self-sufficient. Each one of us, while independent to some degree, depends upon something or someone to exist and to thrive. In Augustine's view, the ultimate Other upon which humanity depends for its existence and sustenance is God. It requires humility in order to recognize our dependence upon God. In those moments of humility and truth, we come to realize that we are not sufficient in ourselves. By recognizing our finitude, we are open to a transcendent being beyond our power to control. It is then that we can cooperate with God's grace to be transformed in charity by the work of the Holy Spirit. The spiritual life is about our encounter with the infinite God for whom we long and with whom we seek to be united in love.

Growth in the spiritual life is a gift of God's grace. God has not abandoned us, nor have we been left to save ourselves. Instead, God has provided the way. God became one of us in the incarnation to redeem our fallen humanity and to offer us a share in divinity. Christ instituted the church and the sacraments to dispense divine grace as medicine for wounded souls. The church is a hospital of healing as the medium of grace and salvation. Our spiritual journey is marked by the gradual healing of our disordered desires so that we might learn to love God, ourselves, and our neighbors properly. We undergo this healing by sharing in the sacraments and by being part of a community defined by charity. By clinging to God in love, we become conformed to what we love, for God is love. For Augustine, the spiritual life means being conformed to the love of God made flesh in the incarnate Christ so that we might be made one in Christ, the head and the members of his body, for eternity.

ORDER OF CHAPTERS

This book provides a map for those seeking the way to God by following the spiritual path laid out by St. Augustine. According to the bishop of Hippo, the way to God is the way of faith, hope, and charity, which requires not only Christian teaching but also communal practice. The spiritual life must be lived in a community that celebrates sacraments and offers works of mercy in order to build up a body united in love. This community is the church, the city of God on pilgrimage in a process of growth and transformation. The church is on a journey to God as the ultimate source of happiness, and spiritual growth is a process of coming to know and love God in this life in order to be united as one body of Christ forever.

The following chapters explore Augustine's spirituality according to his understanding of God, creation, sin, Christ, the church, and the Holy Spirit. Along the way, we will explore common practices of the church in North Africa and the life of Christian worship in Augustine's time, including participation in the sacraments, prayer, and works of mercy. An Augustinian spirituality yields a life of praise and thanksgiving to God. Praising God begins during this life by participation in a communal body, and it will continue for all of eternity, such that heaven will be a life of praise without ceasing. Our journey will end in the enjoyment of God with one another. This is the life of true blessedness that we are all seeking as spiritual creatures on the way to our heavenly homeland.

1

The Journey of the Heart

Desiring God and True Happiness

The entire life of a good Christian is a holy desire.
—Augustine, *Homilies on the First Epistle of John* 4.6

AUGUSTINE IS RIGHTLY DESCRIBED as a theologian of the heart.[1] The earliest Christian authors understood the heart to be the hidden center of the human person and the inner seat of decision and desire. For Augustine, the heart is an image of desire. We are spiritual creatures who live and move according to what we desire and what we love. However, we seldom take time to reflect on what we desire the most. Instead, we occupy ourselves with satisfying immediate, fleeting, and superficial wants. An Augustinian spirituality invites us to explore our deepest desires by asking what we long for at the deepest level of our being. What do we desire above all things? What, or whom, do we love with our whole heart?

By contemplating our deepest desires, we discover that we are made for more than temporary gratification. We are always searching for something, or someone, that transcends the material world around us. The human heart can find rest only in a spiritual source and a transcendent end. According to Augustine,

1. Martin, *Our Restless Heart*, 41.

this spiritual reality is what Christians call God. In the opening lines of *The Confessions*, Augustine famously addresses God as the one who has created us and drawn us to himself, so that we can find proper rest in him. "Great are you, O Lord, and exceedingly worthy of praise. . . . You arouse us so that praising you may bring us joy, because you have made us and drawn us to yourself, and our heart is unquiet until it rests in you."[2] Our spiritual journey is marked by restlessness of heart, a constant reminder that true rest can be found only in God.

The spiritual life is a journey of the heart to God. We are all on journey in pursuit of eternal happiness. During our earthly journey, we experience restlessness of the heart. This restlessness is a universal experience. If we listen carefully to our hearts, we will find that we desire something beyond this world. In Augustine's view, our experience of desire can lead us on a quest for true happiness, which can be fulfilled only in God.

All human beings seek happiness. The problem is that we look for happiness in the wrong places. We might try to satisfy the longing of our hearts by indulging in physical pleasures or puffing ourselves up with pride. These misguided efforts inevitably lead to disappointment, dissatisfaction, and misery. We find true happiness only by allowing our desire to lead us to God, so that we can cling to him in love. Only in God do we find the rest we are desperately seeking.

Our restless heart reminds us that we depend entirely upon God. We do not exist in isolation; we are made for union with God and others. Our desires can serve as signs pointing us toward God. All things have been made by God and for God. According to Augustine, the spiritual life involves learning to order our desires properly so that we can be drawn to God as our ultimate rest. An Augustinian spirituality of the heart is not about turning inward to find our own truth apart from God. Instead, by turning inward, we realize we are meant to turn outward to God, who is truth itself and the source of our happiness.

2. Augustine, *Confessions* 1.1.1.

In this chapter, we will explore Augustine's complex understanding of desire and how our experience of desire can lead us to an awareness of God. First, we will examine Augustine's view of the heart as the inner human being. By turning inward, we uncover the source of our desire for happiness, which is nothing other than the desire for God. Then, we can learn how to direct our desire toward God, who has created us for himself. If indeed we are led to God by desire, then the question arises: What or who is God? We will analyze Augustine's doctrine of God, as it developed in different contexts. Finally, we will consider what it means to love God with the heart. In Augustine's spirituality, the practice of turning inward to the heart naturally leads us to ascend upward to God and to turn outward toward others in love.

As a master of the spiritual life, Augustine reminds us that nothing in this world can satisfy the deepest longing of our heart. However, this does not mean that the good things we encounter in the world are evil. On the contrary, all things are created good by God. Due to our fallen condition, we often desire good things incorrectly, that is, apart from or against God. The Christian life involves learning how to have a holy desire, so that we can love God above all things. Then, we can begin to love all things in God, that is, with God as our end and final goal. As we grow in the spiritual life, we learn how to receive all good things as gifts that lead us to a deeper love of God, the giver of all good gifts. By embarking on this journey, we discover that true happiness and rest are found in God, who alone satisfies the deepest desire of the human heart.

THE HEART

An Augustinian spirituality can be characterized as a spirituality of the heart.[3] Most often, when Augustine speaks of the heart, or *cor* in Latin, he is referring to the inner human being. The heart represents the inner spiritual soul, as distinct from the outer material body. Although the soul and body are distinct, they are not

3. J. Smith, *On the Road with Augustine*, 13.

entirely separate, for together they form one human nature. The heart is the spiritual soul of the human being. Following Paul in 2 Cor 4:16, Augustine identifies the heart as the interior human being that is being renewed every day, while the exterior human being is wasting away. The heart is the center of spiritual renewal and transformation by grace. The heart can guide us toward God, because God works within us to renew and transform the inner human being.

In his many theological works, Augustine often uses the word "heart" to refer to the intellect or the will, which are distinct yet inseparable. The spiritual soul includes both the intellect and the will, without being reduced to either. As spiritual creatures, humans are capable of knowledge and love through the mind and the will, respectively. Sometimes, when Augustine mentions the heart, he is referring specifically to the intellect or the mind's desire for truth.[4] Other times, he uses the image of the heart to represent the will, which desires the good.[5] Although he can use the heart in these particular ways, overall, the heart symbolizes the entire spiritual soul with its operations of knowing and loving.

One key aspect of Augustine's view of the heart as the inner human being is that it never exists independently. The human is not an isolated "self" that is completely autonomous and self-sufficient.[6] Instead, all people depend on God for their existence, as God is the source of all being. Whether we realize it or not, we rely on God at all times. We are dependent spiritual creatures by nature. God is the foundation of our very existence. As human beings, we live and move because God sustains us and grants us the gift of life.

Additionally, as Augustine teaches, human beings are inherently social, relational, and communal. No one is an island. Regardless of our circumstances, we exist in relation to God, creation, and others. The social nature of human beings is evident in the opening passage of *The Confessions*, in which Augustine states

4. Augustine, *Letter* 41.1.

5. Augustine, *True Religion* 11.24.

6. Cavadini, *Visioning Augustine*, 138–55.

that "our heart" is restless until it rests in God. Augustine uses the singular form of "heart" (*cor*) and the plural pronoun "our" (*nostrum*) to indicate that we share one human nature and form one body.[7] Although we are many individuals, we are created as a communal body. When Augustine talks about the heart, he has both the individual and the community in mind.[8]

GOD AND THE HEART

The heart is constantly in motion in the pursuit of truth and goodness. We are always drawn to seek the truth and love what is good. Since God is the source of all truth and goodness, the heart is always in pursuit of God. According to Augustine, the intellect and will are operations of the soul that attract the person toward God. Just as the physical heart pumps blood and maintains a pulse through the body, the spiritual soul is also always in motion. In a treatise on the nature of the soul, Augustine says that when Scripture speaks of loving God with "our whole heart," this "does not refer to the part of our flesh that lies behind the ribs, but to the power that produces thoughts . . . as the motion in the heart that carries the pulse through all the veins never stops, so we turn something over in our thought without ceasing."[9] The heart is an image of the intellectual soul, which has the power to generate thought and is constantly seeking truth. The spiritual soul is dynamic, always searching for the truth that leads to God.

God is the truth and goodness that we seek with our heart. As Augustine understands it, God can be present to the human person in a unique way.[10] No created thing can be as present and intimate to a human being as God. For God sees the thoughts of everyone, and God knows the human heart. "God sees the thoughts

7. Augustine, *Confessions* 1.1.1.
8. Irizar and Dupont, "Many as One," 6.
9. Augustine, *Nature of the Soul* 4.6.7.
10. Augustine, *Exposition of Psalm* 141.4.

of everyone; this is what the word heart means."[11] The heart is the entire "inner human being," where God can be present.[12] It is not a physical space, but rather the heart is where God comes to dwell. For Augustine, God is closer and more intimate to us than we are to ourselves, for God knows the depths of the human heart.

Likewise, Augustine asserts that God dwells within the inner conscience of the person. God can guide the inner human being in ways no creature can. "Thus [God] guides the just person's conscience in his own presence, guides it in the place where no human being sees; he alone sees who discerns what each person thinks and what causes each person delight."[13] God knows the desires of our heart. "Therefore the one who examines the heart sees the things which we really care about. But he who explores our inward parts sees also the object of our striving and where we seek our joy."[14] During our earthly journey, God is already present in our conscience, and God alone sees all of our thoughts. Even the sinner knows that God is present to the heart. "But God is present there, isn't he? Assuredly, but in the sinner's outlook there is no room for the fear of God."[15] We cannot see the hearts of others, for our hearts are like dark clouds.[16] Yet God sees the heart and the "inner act of the will."[17] God speaks in secret to the heart and says to the soul, "I am your salvation."[18] God is the owner of the heart and dwells in the inmost being of the person.[19] God also hears the cry of the heart, for "your inner thoughts are your clamor in the Lord's hearing."[20] God is present to the heart as the ultimate object of our love.

11. Augustine, *Exposition of Psalm* 7.9.
12. Augustine, *Letter* 121.3.18.
13. Augustine, *Exposition of Psalm* 7.9.
14. Augustine, *Exposition of Psalm* 7.9.
15. Augustine, *Exposition of Psalm* 35.2.
16. Augustine, *Exposition of Psalm* 55.9; 88[1].7.
17. Augustine, *Spirit and the Letter* 8.14.
18. Augustine, *Exposition of Psalm* 38.20.
19. Augustine, *Exposition of Psalm* 138.18.
20. Augustine, *Exposition of Psalm* 141.2.

According to Augustine, the true object of our heart's deepest desire is God. Yet, we often forget this truth. We become distracted by pursuing other goods, which fail to satisfy the inner longing of the human heart. This can become a serious obstacle on our path to God, because God should be the ultimate focus of our love and our deepest joy. Augustine teaches that spiritual life is a gradual process of learning how to desire God rightly. Ultimately, all good things should lead us to the good God. If we look inward and carefully examine our hearts, we will find that our desire for happiness is nothing less than a desire for God. Since everyone desires happiness, we can start our journey to God by turning to the heart.

THE JOURNEY OF THE HEART

In *The Confessions*, Augustine describes his spiritual odyssey as a journey of the heart. This journey is not taken by foot, but rather through the affections of the heart. "It was a journey not to be undertaken by ship or carriage or on foot . . . for to travel—and more, to reach journey's end—was nothing else but to want to go there, [and] to want it valiantly and with all my heart."[21] The journey of the heart is a quest driven by desire. Augustine often compares the spiritual journey to sailing on stormy seas. We are like sailors on a dangerous voyage, trying to find our way home. "Isn't this whole earth like a great ship carrying its crew and passengers over the tossing waves, in great danger, subject to so many squalls and storms? They are afraid of shipwreck, they are longing to reach port, but at least they already realize they are travelers on a journey."[22] We are all travelers on journey in this world, searching for our way home.

In some of his early works, Augustine describes different classes of seafarers who progress based on their pursuit of wisdom. Those who have advanced in philosophy stay near the port and give signs for others to find their way home. Some are misled by

21. Augustine, *Confessions* 8.8.19.

22. Augustine, *Sermon* 346C.2.

false appearances and venture far away. Finally, others are tossed about by storms, but they still perceive signs and remember the wonderful sweetness of home. Many of us fall into this last group. We face storms while on our journey, yet we can still see signs that point us back home.

What is our homeland, and what signs can help us find our way home? According to Augustine, our homeland is nothing less than heaven, and our desires serve as the signs guiding us in the right direction. Our longing to know the truth and to love the good will lead us to our spiritual home with God. As we continue to seek truth and goodness, we can begin making progress on the journey to our heavenly homeland.

As Augustine notes, during our journey, we cannot see God with our physical eyes. However, we can start to see God with the heart insofar as we gaze upon truth with the inner mind's eye. As we begin to understand truth, we start our spiritual journey. "For this is a journey which is made not by any change of geographical location on earth, but with the desires of our minds."[23] We are on the path to God through our mind's desire, which leads to a vision of truth. Since God is truth, we can begin to see God by desiring and attaining truth.

However, our spiritual journey is not based purely on reason. That is, it is not simply an intellectual exercise, as if learning philosophy alone can guide us home. Instead, Augustine emphasizes that, as spiritual creatures, we must undergo a transformation of our affections or loves so we can cling to truth and goodness. This involves transforming the will, because our journey is "not from place to place, but one traveled by the affections."[24] Just as the mind seeks truth as its object of knowledge, so too the will seeks the good as its object of love. Since God is truth and goodness itself, God is the proper object of our knowledge and love.

Yet, many obstacles stand in our way. We can easily lose our way. We need proper vessels that will help us return to our homeland so that we are no longer exiles living in unhappiness. We must

23. Augustine, *Exposition of Psalm* 5.11.

24. Augustine, *Teaching Christianity* 1.17.16.

also direct our desires to God instead of becoming enamored with the beauty of this world. The problem is that we can become captivated by the objects of the journey and the experience of being at sea. Augustine says it is like being on a cruise ship and enjoying the experience while forgetting our final destination. We can lose sight of the fact that our true homeland is God. "But if they love traveling, they forget home, and don't want to go back. Our true home is not such that we should put anything else before it."[25] While on the journey, we tend to cling to worldly things as if they were the source of our true happiness. As a result, our way home is "blocked, as by a barricade of thorn bushes, by the malice of our past sins."[26] To make progress, the heart must undergo a transformation of affections. We need to learn how to let go of worldly attachments and cling to God instead. By becoming fixated on material things, we are blocked from our spiritual home.

In a sermon on the meaning of Pentecost, Augustine highlights that a major obstacle on our spiritual journey is attachment to wealth and riches. "Sometimes, you see, while people are traveling, they get rich. They were needy at home, they travel and become rich, and don't want to go back."[27] Even though we are born in a state of traveling away from God, we must remember that our true homeland is heaven. "As for us, we were all born traveling a long way away from our Lord. . . . Our home country is in heaven. . . . May the world grow cheap in our eyes, may we learn to love and prefer the one by whom the world was made."[28] Christ has promised the gift of the Holy Spirit to guide us back home, but our attachment to riches can prevent us from returning to our home country. The gifts of the Holy Spirit are given to teach us to love God and to prefer the creator over the created world.

To be clear, the preference for God does not mean denying the goodness of the created world, for all good gifts come from the good God. However, Augustine teaches that the good things

25. Augustine, *Sermon* 378.1.

26. Augustine, *Teaching Christianity* 1.17.16.

27. Augustine, *Sermon* 378.1.

28. Augustine, *Sermon* 378.1.

of this world are meant to be used temporarily. No created thing is our final end or destiny. On our spiritual journey, we must learn to make use of this world as travelers do with an inn—temporarily. "Make use of this world, do not be taken in by the world. You entered the world, you are making a journey, you came intending to leave, not to stay; you are a wayfarer; this life is a wayside inn."[29] We are wayfarers on the path to our heavenly homeland. Meanwhile, we should use wealth and riches as travelers on the road. "Use money in the way a traveler at a wayside inn uses the table, the cups, the pitcher, the bed—intending to leave, not to stay."[30] Instead of clinging to wealth, we should deposit treasures in heaven by lifting our hearts upward. "So if our fortunes are buried in the ground, our thoughts will drag our hearts downward. But if they are in a heavenly savings deposit, our hearts will be lifted upward. . . . So if any of you really want to lift up your hearts, then it's up there that you must deposit what you love. . . . Our earthly home is falling into ruin, our heavenly home is eternal."[31] By lifting our hearts to heaven, we can make a deposit that has eternal value. While this world and its riches are temporary, our heavenly home is everlasting.

For Augustine, our spiritual journey involves learning how to use earthly and material things to lead us toward the enjoyment of God's eternal and spiritual truths. All the beautiful things in the world are meant to guide us to cling to God, who has created all beautiful things. "We shall never be able to understand how beautiful, how great, how worthy of God, how—finally—true is that which we seek unless we begin from things that are human and close by."[32] The beautiful things of this life should not be rejected; instead, we can channel our love for these things to God, who is deserving of all love. "If sensuous beauty delights you, praise God for the beauty of corporeal things, and channel the love you feel for them onto their Maker, lest the things that please you lead you

29. Augustine, *Homilies on Gospel of John* 40.10.

30. Augustine, *Homilies on Gospel of John* 40.10.

31. Augustine, *Sermon* 86.1.

32. Augustine, *Catholic and Manichean Way* 1.7.12.

to displease him."[33] Since God has made all beautiful things, we should love God and accept all things as good gifts from him.

One problem with our current condition is that we tend to place God's gifts above the Giver. We often love things more than God, instead of allowing them to lead us to him. This is what it means to be "worldly," according to Augustine. The lovers of the world keep their hearts rooted in the world instead of raising them to heaven. "For all lovers of the world, because they inhabit the world by their love, just as they inhabit heaven whose hearts are above and who walk on the earth in their flesh—all lovers of the world, therefore, are called 'the world.'"[34] In this context, "the world" does not simply refer to the created world, which is inherently good. Rather, the worldly are those who are defined by the lust of the flesh, the lust of the eyes, and the pride of life, as explained in the biblical text 1 John 2:16. "They have nothing but these three things, the desire of the flesh, the desire of the eyes and the ambition of the world, for they desire to eat, to drink, to have sexual intercourse—to use these pleasures."[35] Worldliness means clinging to worldly things and pleasures instead of clinging to God.

This is exactly how Augustine describes sin at the end of book 1 of *The Confessions*. "In this lay my sin, that not in [God] was I seeking pleasures, distinctions, and truth, but in myself and the rest of his creatures, and so I fell headlong into pains, confusions, and errors."[36] Earlier in the same passage, Augustine emphasizes that all created things are gifts from God. "In a living creature such as this everything is wonderful and worthy of praise, but all these things are gifts from God."[37] Sin does not stem from the gifts themselves or even from enjoying the pleasures of the world, but from taking pleasure in such things over and against God. Sin causes a division and separation between the creator and creation. Worldly people misuse the things of the world and cling to them instead of

33. Augustine, *Confessions* 4.12.18.

34. Augustine, *Homilies on First Epistle of John* 2.12.

35. Augustine, *Homilies on First Epistle of John* 2.12.

36. Augustine, *Confessions* 1.20.31.

37. Augustine, *Confessions* 1.20.31.

to God. Those who truly follow God, however, make progress on their spiritual journey by directing their love for all things toward God, who is the giver of every good gift.

One of Augustine's greatest spiritual insights is that nothing in the world can satisfy our deepest longing. No temporary or material possession can fulfill our desire for true and lasting happiness. All humans want to be happy, but not everyone knows how to become happy. According to Augustine, we can follow our desire for happiness to arrive at God. Thus, the desire for happiness can serve as a guiding light on the path to God, who alone fulfills our desire for eternal happiness.

DESIRING TRUE HAPPINESS

Every human being seeks what Augustine calls the "happy life" (*beata vita*), or the life of blessedness. We live in constant pursuit of true happiness. This is essential to our human nature, for we desire happiness above all else. "Every human being, though, of whatever kind or quality, wishes to be happy. There isn't anybody who doesn't want that, and want it in such a way as to want it above everything else."[38] However, not everyone knows how to be happy. "Ask any people whether they wish to be happy, and they will answer without the slightest hesitation that they do. They all cry out that they want to be happy; but how to get to that happiness, and where that happiness is to be found, this they don't know; that's why they go wrong."[39] Too often, we pursue different longings as if they will satisfy our deepest desires. Different longings carry us away, and although "one longs for this, another for that . . . a happy life is the common aim of all."[40] All people, good or bad, seek to be happy, even if some speculate wrongly about what constitutes happiness. "This appetite for the blessed life is common to philosophers and Christians . . . it is characteristic of everybody, absolutely

38. Augustine, *Sermon* 306.3.

39. Augustine, *Sermon* 346B.2.

40. Augustine, *Sermon* 306.3.

everybody, good and bad alike. People who are good, after all, are good in order to be happy, and those who are bad would not be bad unless they hoped they could thereby be made happy."[41] The motive behind every action in this life is to arrive at happiness. "Whatever people do, good or bad, their motive is always to get rid of their misery and win happiness; invariably they want to be happy. People who lead good lives and people who lead bad lives, they all want to be happy; but what they all want does not come the way of all."[42] The desire for true happiness is a universal, but not everyone attains a happy life.

Augustine claims that many people seek after things that will not make them happy, such as material goods or pleasures. "I know you all want to live happy lives. But what is it that makes a person's life happy? . . . You are seeking gold, because you imagine you will be happy with gold; but gold doesn't make one happy."[43] Neither wealth nor the enjoyment of material things will make one truly happy. It is a mistake to think that material things are themselves the source of happiness. "Whatever has given them the greatest enjoyment constitutes, they have decided, the happy life. How in this case can everyone love so fervently what not everyone knows? Who can love what he does not know. . . . So how is it that happiness is loved by all and yet not known by all?"[44] Since everyone wants happiness, but not everyone knows how to be happy, how can one love what one does not know?

Augustine addresses this question by focusing on the pursuit of truth. We are all constantly seeking truth, even if we do not fully know it or possess it entirely. Despite our ignorance, we are all capable of receiving and embracing truth. All of us desire truth, for no one wants to be deceived. By seeking and finding truth, we discover the happy life. "Add truth to life, and you find the happy life. Nobody, after all, wants to be deceived, just as nobody wants

41. Augustine, *Sermon* 150.4.

42. Augustine, *Exposition of Psalm* 32[3].15.

43. Augustine, *Sermon* 231.4.

44. Augustine, *Trinity* 13.4.7.

to die."[45] God is truth, and those who seek to know and love the truth are seeking God. By sincerely desiring truth, we are guided to eternal life with God. "Eternal life, then, is the knowledge of the truth. . . . What, then, are we to do? What, I ask, but first desire with full love him whom we want to know?"[46] Although our knowledge of God is limited, we can begin to know and love God by seeking and striving for truth. Those who attain truth are those who enjoy the blessed life.[47] Ultimately, the supreme measure of truth is God. Therefore, to be truly blessed or happy means to "enjoy God."[48] The pursuit of happiness is, in fact, the pursuit of God. Or as Augustine puts it, the pursuit of God is the desire for happiness, but the attainment of God is happiness itself.[49]

For Augustine, the happy life is not reducible to an intellectual exercise. True happiness is not simply a matter of attaining knowledge, for it also requires loving the good. "For it is not the person who merely knows the good that is justifiably called good; it is rather the person who loves the good."[50] To be happy, one must learn to want what is good and to love the good. "All desire happiness, yet in order to be happy, one must love and pursue what is good, not what is bad. The happy person is one who both has the good things he wants and does not want any bad things."[51] Happiness can be achieved only when it is appropriately desired. "Thus no one is happy but the man who has everything he wants, and wants nothing wrongly."[52] Two things are required to be happy, namely, "to wish well and to be able to do what you wish."[53] The will must be directed toward what is truly good to attain happiness. The happy life, therefore, is a life lived well or justly. "All want

45. Augustine, *Sermon* 306.9.

46. Augustine, *Catholic and Manichean Way* 1.25.47.

47. Augustine, *Happy Life* 4.34.

48. Augustine, *Happy Life* 4.34.

49. Augustine, *Catholic and Manichean Way* 1.11.18.

50. Augustine, *City of God* 11.28.

51. Augustine, *Trinity* 13.6.9.

52. Augustine, *Trinity* 13.5.8.

53. Augustine, *Trinity* 13.13.17.

happiness, but the only ones who will get it are those who want to be just."[54] In the end, the happy life consists of attaining truth and loving the good.

The spiritual life involves making progress toward the object of our deepest desire. The object of our love must be helpful and not harmful, for we cannot be happy if what we have is detrimental to us. "We certainly all want to live happily. . . . But, from my perspective, a person cannot be said to be happy who does not have what he loves, whatever it might be. Nor can he be said to be happy who has what he loves if it is harmful."[55] Growth in happiness is a process that requires learning how to love the greatest good. For "someone who desires what he cannot obtain is tormented, and someone who has obtained what he ought not to have desired is deceived, and someone who does not desire what he ought to desire is sick."[56] In order to be happy, one must learn how to love and enjoy the highest good. "After all, what else is it that we call enjoyment but to have present what you love? No one is happy who does not enjoy that which is the highest good of a human being."[57]

What is the greatest good for a human being? Augustine answers that it is none other than God, for God is the supreme truth and goodness. True happiness, therefore, consists of knowing and loving God. "Now the happy life is joy in the truth; and that means joy in you, who are the Truth, O God. . . . Everyone wants this happy life . . . and when they love the happy life, which is nothing else but joy in the truth, they are unquestionably loving truth also."[58] God is the source of happiness, and God is the source of all good things. "God is the only source to be found of any good things, but especially of those which make a man good and those which will make him happy; only from him do they come into

54. Augustine, *Exposition of Psalm* 32[3].15.

55. Augustine, *Catholic and Manichean Way* 1.2.4.

56. Augustine, *Catholic and Manichean Way* 1.2.4.

57. Augustine, *Catholic and Manichean Way* 1.2.4.

58. Augustine, *Confessions* 10.22.33.

a man and attach themselves to a man."[59] To be happy means to rejoice in truth and life, and this means to find joy in God.

THE ASCENT TO GOD

One key insight from Augustine's spirituality is that happiness is not found simply by turning inward, for the greatest good for all human beings cannot be found in the soul itself. Instead, true happiness can be found only by the ascent to God, who is the happiness of the soul. "When it is happy, the soul itself is not happy because of its own good," for the soul is truly happy when "it strives to cling to God and to be re-created and re-formed by that immutable being."[60] Happiness requires a process of being transformed in truth and goodness through the encounter with God. The soul becomes unhappier the more it wanders away from God and seeks temporary pleasures and happiness in the things of this world. "The soul, then, is filled with folly and unhappiness the farther it wanders off from God to things lower than itself not by place but by love and desire. It returns to God, therefore, by the love by which it desires not to make itself equal to God but to make itself subject to him."[61] The soul's happiness is found beyond itself in God, and only by ascending to God can human beings discover their highest and greatest good.

The soul makes progress on the ascent to God by desiring a life of service, for serving God leads to eternal life. Just as everyone wants truth in order to be happy, so too everyone wants life. "So there is no life that deserves the name, to be called life, but a blessed life; and there can be no blessed life that is not eternal. This is what everybody wants, this is what we all want: truth and life."[62] All creatures desire eternal life, even those who are not religious, for even the godless desire immortality, "but it is indeed a great

59. Augustine, *Trinity* 13.7.10.

60. Augustine, *Letter* 118.3.15.

61. Augustine, *Catholic and Manichean Way* 1.12.21.

62. Augustine, *Sermon* 150.4.

thing to believe that we shall be immortal, and to live in such a way that we are able to attain to that immortality."[63] God himself is the life that brings us happiness, while this worldly life in itself does not suffice. The beautiful things of this life can direct us toward the beauty of the next life if we live in service to God. "Let us love the beauty of that life. . . . God himself is this very life. . . . Let us love this life with all our might."[64] By seeking to love and serve God, we are transformed into the likeness of God's own life of love. And if we genuinely desire eternal life, we will discover that our deepest desire is for God, who is eternal life.

Augustine offers timeless wisdom about human nature and our absolute dependence upon God. We are all finite creatures seeking everlasting life. Augustine teaches us that this very life comes from God, who is the source of all life. When we seek the happiness of eternal life, we are seeking God; and when we seek God, we are seeking the life of happiness. "When I seek you, my God, what I am seeking is a life of happiness."[65] God himself is the source of our life as spiritual creatures, for God gives life to the soul just as the soul gives life to the body. "Let me seek you that my soul may live, for as my body draws its life from my soul, so does my soul draw its life from you."[66] God is the unchangeable and immutable source of all things that change. "There is a nature mutable in terms of places and of times, such as a body. There is also a nature mutable in no way in terms of places, but only in terms of times, such as the soul. And there is a nature which cannot be changed either in terms of places or in terms of times; this is God."[67] God is the first principle and foundation of all that exists. In order to be truly happy, spiritual creatures seek not only life but also truth and immortality. "All people then want to be happy; they want something true, this necessarily means they want to be

63. Augustine, *Sermon* 335H.1.

64. Augustine, *Sermon* 302.7.

65. Augustine, *Confessions* 10.20.29.

66. Augustine, *Confessions* 10.20.29.

67. Augustine, *Letter* 18.2.

immortal. They cannot otherwise be happy."[68] To be happy means finding joy in God, who is everlasting truth. "Now the happy life is joy in the truth; and that means joy in you, who are the Truth, O God who shed the light of salvation on my face, my God."[69] Since true happiness is found in God, we are restless apart from him. The spiritual life involves turning inward so that by examining our restless heart, we can be led upward to God, who is the source of truth, happiness, and eternal life.

MY LOVE IS MY WEIGHT

But how can we enjoy God if we do not yet know him? As Augustine declares in *The Confessions*, "Which comes first. . . . To know you or to call upon you? Must we know you before we can call upon you?"[70] While he does not offer a simple answer to these questions, Augustine reflects on how we are drawn to God by our loves, just as material objects are drawn by their weight. The pull of a body's weight "is, in a way, its love, whether it tries to sink downward due to its heaviness or rise upward due to its lightness. For a body is drawn by its weight, just as a soul is drawn by its love wherever it is drawn."[71] The soul is carried by its love as if by a weight. "The mind is, of course, carried by its love as if by a weight wherever it is carried; we are commanded, therefore, to take away from the weight of desire what is added to the weight of love until the former is done away with and the latter is made perfect."[72] Our desires must be purified so that we can arrive at the ultimate object of our love, which is none other than God.

68. Augustine, *Trinity* 13.8.11.

69. Augustine, *Confessions* 10.22.33. According to Romano Guardini, "Viewed in context with Augustine's teachings on man, this submerging of a human existence in divine truth is the supreme spiritual life" (*Conversion of Augustine*, 5).

70. Augustine, *Confessions* 1.1.1.

71. Augustine, *City of God* 11.28.

72. Augustine, *Letter* 157.9.

Augustine challenges us to examine our desires so that we can order them properly toward God. As human beings, our existence is marked by a profound longing. Our lives are filled with restlessness because we cannot find satisfaction in any material thing. Love of this world or this life is not enough. "What have you fallen in love with, and what are you in love with? Where has it got you?"[73] We experience restlessness and dissatisfaction the more we attempt to find fulfillment within the material world. True love leads us beyond ourselves to our transcendent end, which is where we find our rest. "Our true place is where we find rest. We are borne toward it by love."[74] Love moves us in the direction toward which it intends.[75] Love charts a course toward a particular end, and our ultimate end and resting place is God. We find our rest in God because God is the source of our true happiness and our final good.[76] Only in the transcendent God do we find the fulfillment of our deepest longing for love.

Whether we are aware of it or not, we spend our lives in pursuit of our transcendent end. Augustine explains that weight is a force "within each thing that seems to make it strain toward its proper place."[77] Just as material things tend toward their proper ends, so human beings tend toward their proper end in God. Fire is borne upward, and likewise, God's church strains toward heaven. Christ ascended to heaven so that the church might be pulled upward to heaven.[78] The weight of charity enables the church to reach the kingdom of immortality.[79] Our desire for eternal life is fulfilled only by clinging to God in love and ascending to our final resting place.

If indeed God is our transcendent end and final rest, the question arises—what or who is God? What do we mean when

73. Augustine, *Sermon* 302.6.

74. Augustine, *Confessions* 13.9.10.

75. Augustine, *Exposition of Psalm* 9.14.

76. Augustine, *Confessions* 1.4.4—1.5.5.

77. Augustine, *Exposition of Psalm* 29[2].10.

78. Augustine, *Sermon* 337.4.

79. Augustine, *Sermon* 228.2.

we speak about God? Augustine's doctrine of God is most helpful because of its articulation of the divine attributes and the relationship between creator and creatures. His view of God informs his understanding of the spiritual life, for the aim of the spiritual life is a transformative encounter with the living God.

AUGUSTINE'S DOCTRINE OF GOD

Augustine's understanding of God developed over his lifetime, especially after Augustine rejected Manicheism. Contrary to the false claims of the Manicheans, Augustine came to see God as immaterial, infinite, and all-powerful. Following the philosophy of Platonism, he concluded that evil is not coeternal with God, because that would make God weak and limited. Instead, God is the source of all being, truth, and goodness. God is the light of truth itself, eternal and indivisible, and therefore, God is not subject to division or corruption. The world is an ordered cosmos that exists by participation in God, who is the source of all being.[80]

Platonism heavily influenced Augustine's doctrine of God, but it took its final shape during his conversion to Christianity. This is evident in book 1 of *The Confessions*, in which Augustine asks what God is. "What are you then, my God [*Quid es*]?"[81] Augustine's answer to the question follows a Platonic formula. "Are you not everywhere in your whole being [*Ubique totus es*]?"[82] Since God is being itself, God alone can be everywhere at once, without suffering any loss or change. This view of the divine resembles the Platonic God, who is "most high, excellent, most powerful, omnipotent."[83] But when Augustine asks, "What are you to me?" God is the source of salvation and mercy. "What are you to me [*Quid es mihi*]? Have mercy on me, so that I may tell. . . . Through your own merciful dealings with me, O Lord my God,

80. Chadwick, *Augustine of Hippo*, 22.

81. Augustine, *Confessions* 1.4.4.

82. Augustine, *Confessions* 1.3.3.

83. Augustine, *Confessions* 1.4.4.

tell me what you are to me. Say to my soul, *I am your salvation*."[84] God is not an impersonal force; rather, God is "supremely merciful and supremely just, most hidden yet intimately present."[85] God is the source of life, health, and salvation. "Everything I need for health and salvation flows from my God."[86] For Augustine, God is not simply the impersonal One of Platonism, from whom all being flows. Instead, God is the personal creator and merciful redeemer of humanity. Human beings have been created in God's image and likeness (Gen 1:26–27), and all are made for union and communion with God, who is the source of healing and salvation.

Augustine's view of God is rooted in his interpretation of Scripture. The Old Testament reveals that God is the source of all existence. God's very nature is to be. Noting that God's self-declared name in Exod 3:14 is "I Am Who Am," Augustine concludes that God is "called Being-Itself, as though that were his name. . . . His very nature is to be, and so true is this that, when compared with him, all created things are as though they had no being."[87] Since God is being itself and transcends creation, God can be intimately present to all creatures, for only God can be everywhere whole at once. This idea demonstrates the harmony between Platonic philosophy and Christian theology. The Christian can find peace and rest in God, for God is uniquely present to the soul. "And that is why the person of faith rejoices and says, *In peace, in Being-Itself, I will rest and fall asleep*, leaving aside those many people who are completely fragmented by their desire for temporal things and ask, *Who has anything good to show us?*"[88] Augustine's interpretation of Exodus forms the basis of his theology of the divine.

Further, God is simple insofar as God is one and unchangeable.[89] This distinguishes the simple God from his creation. "What I have here said is mutable in some way is called a creature; what

84. Augustine, *Confessions* 1.5.5.
85. Augustine, *Confessions* 1.4.4.
86. Augustine, *Confessions* 1.6.7.
87. Augustine, *Exposition of Psalm* 134.4.
88. Augustine, *Exposition of Psalm* 4.9.
89. Augustine, *City of God* 11.10.

is immutable is the creator."[90] Since God is one in being and one in spirit, God cannot be divided into parts. "It was once said in terms of substance that *God is spirit*."[91] As one divine substance, God is spirit and life. All spiritual creatures find their source in God by participating in spirit. "For in the scriptures this term 'spirit,' not insofar as it is relative but insofar as it signifies a nature, refers to every incorporeal nature of spirit; for this reason this term applies not only to the Father, the Son, and the Holy Spirit but to every rational creature and soul."[92] God created rational creatures, including angels and human beings, to share in his life. Since God is the source of life, God is the source of all goodness and happiness for human beings. "That highest being is happiness itself; the lowest is what can be neither happy nor unhappy."[93] God is the highest being in whom truth, beauty, and goodness are found in the maximal degree. Only union with God can bring true happiness to spiritual creatures made in God's image and likeness.

In the Christian tradition, God is not only the one unchangeable source of life and truth, but God is also triune. According to Augustine, the doctrine of the Trinity is an invitation to communion with three divine persons, Father, Son, and Holy Spirit, who are united as one God. As Augustine puts it, God is one, yet God is a triple oneness. "Hence, we ought to love God, a certain triple oneness, Father, Son, and Holy Spirit, and I shall say that God is nothing other than being itself."[94] The three persons of the Trinity are distinct in relation and not in substance. This distinction does not introduce division into the divine nature, but rather reveals how God is a communion of love. The greatest good for human beings is to enter into communion with the triune God and to cling to God in love. "For what else will be the greatest good for a human being but he to whom it is most blessed to cling. But that is God alone, to whom we can certainly only cling by longing, desire, and

90. Augustine, *Letter* 18.2.

91. Augustine, *Letter* 238.15.

92. Augustine, *Letter* 238.15.

93. Augustine, *Letter* 18.2.

94. Augustine, *Catholic and Manichean Way* 1.14.24.

love."[95] The Trinity reveals that God is love and that human beings find true happiness by clinging to God in love.

SEEING GOD

If God is the one transcendent source of spirit, life, and happiness, how can we cling to God while remaining both spiritual and material creatures? How can we see God if God does not have a material body? According to Augustine, the invisible God is rightly contemplated by gazing upon visible creation. "God's invisible reality is contemplated through things that are created. Gaze at these created things, wonder at them, and seek their maker."[96] God is beauty itself, which can be glimpsed by contemplating the beauty of creation. "Surely this beauty is apparent to all whose faculties are sound? Human beings have the power to question, so that by understanding the things he has made they may glimpse the unseen things of God."[97] All visible things can direct our hearts to the invisible God, who made all things. In this way, we can use the things of the world to guide us to God, the source of all existence, but we should not set our heart on the things of this world. "We too make use of them according to the needs of our journey; but we don't set our heart's joy on them, in case when they collapse we should be buried in the ruins."[98] God is the source of the heart's joy and true happiness, not any created thing.

Augustine lays out a map of how we can move from wonder at the beauty of creation to wonder at God in book 10 of *The Confessions*.[99]

Likewise, in his exposition of Ps 41, Augustine declares,

> I look for my God in every bodily creature, whether on earth or in the sky, but I do not find him. I look for his

95. Augustine, *Catholic and Manichean Way* 1.14.24.

96. Augustine, *Exposition of Psalm* 99.6.

97. Augustine, *Confessions* 10.6.10.

98. Augustine, *Sermon* 157.5.

99. Augustine, *Confessions* 10.6.8–9.

> substance in my own soul, but do not find him there. Yet still I have pondered on this search for my God and, longing to gaze on the invisible realities of God by understanding them through created things, I poured out my soul above myself; and now there is nothing left for me to touch, except my God. For there, above my soul, is the home of my God; there he dwells, from there he looks down upon me, from there he created me, from there he governs me and takes thought for me, from there he arouses me, calls me, guides me and leads me on, and from there he will lead me to journey's end.[100]

Human beings can come to see God by gazing upon the beauty of creation, which draws us upward to God in heaven. For nothing is more beautiful than God, and although creation reflects God's beauty, God remains the transcendent source of beauty and light. "You can find nothing more delightful than God . . . there is nothing more beautiful, nothing more full of light than He is."[101] God dwells in heaven as the creator of all things. From this heavenly dwelling, God draws all spiritual creatures to himself. God calls us to embark on our spiritual journey to our heavenly homeland, where we find our heart's true joy and rest.

During our earthly journey, the vision of God requires the gift of faith, for the human heart can see God by the light of faith. "Our hearts are cleansed by faith for this purpose, for the vision of God is promised to us as a reward of faith."[102] Faith is a gift of grace that elevates the soul to know and love God. Just as we love our friends because they are faithful friends, so too we can learn to love God with faith. "So you love faith in him. If you love faith, the eyes with which faith can be seen are the very eyes with which God can be seen."[103] If we have faith in God, we can love what we do not yet see with our bodily eyes. The reward of faith is to arrive at God, who is himself our greatest reward. "Does this mean

100. Augustine, *Exposition of Psalm* 41.5.

101. Augustine, *Sermon* 385.4.

102. Augustine, *Letter* 92.6.

103. Augustine, *Sermon* 385.4.

that God gives us nothing? Nothing, save himself. God's reward is simply God himself."[104] By receiving the gift of faith, we advance toward loving God with the heart during this life so that we can make progress on the journey to our heavenly homeland.

As we have seen, Augustine's view of the spiritual life involves a constant movement of the heart. By turning inward to the desires of the heart, we realize that only God can fulfill our deepest longing. But the journey doesn't end there, for we must continue to ascend in order to be united with God in love. This inevitably leads outward to the love of neighbor, for charity means love of both God and neighbor. Progress in the spiritual life is reflected by growth in the twofold love of God and neighbor.

LOVING GOD WITH THE HEART

How do we grow in our love for God? According to Augustine, clinging to God in love necessitates a purification of the heart from attachment to worldly things. We can begin to love God properly with our heart by turning away from love of the world. "This is our life—to be exercised through desire. But, to the degree that a holy desire exercises us, we have cut off our desires from love of the world."[105] By no longer clinging to created things, we can exercise our desire for God. We can begin to love God by purifying our hearts from disordered attachments.

To love God with the heart also requires a purification of vices, including "injustice, ill will, falsehood, murder, deceit, and anything else of this sort . . . so that God may be seen."[106] To see the light of God is to see by the eyes of the heart. "But you want to behold the light which is seen by the eyes of the heart, because God is that light itself. . . . Do you aspire to see that light? Make your eye clean, so that you can see it, because *blessed are the clean of heart,*

104. Augustine, *Exposition of Psalm* 72.32.

105. Augustine, *Homilies on First Epistle of John* 4.6.

106. Augustine, *Exposition of Psalm* 5.5.

for they shall see God."[107] Purity of heart is to have a pure conscience in the sight of God, whose "gaze pierces a pure conscience."[108] God comes to dwell in a heart that has been cleansed from sin. "Purify your heart so that he may himself enlighten you, and he whom you invoke may enter it. Be a home for him, and he will be a home for you; let him dwell in you, and you will dwell in him. If you have welcomed him with your heart in this age, he will welcome you with his face when this age is past."[109] Christ comes to dwell in the heart where the light of God's face shines. "You have given joy to my heart . . . it is to be sought within, where the light of God's face is stamped. For Christ dwells in the inner person."[110]

Although God cannot be seen with our bodily eyes, Augustine says that if we love God, we will possess him. "You don't see God. Love, and you have him. . . . He calls out to us, 'Love me and you will have me because you can't even love me unless you already have me.'"[111] To possess God means to cling to him until the end of our journey. "By holding out for the Lord you will come to possess him; the one for whom you are holding out will be yours forever. Long for something else, if you can find something greater, better or more lovely!"[112] Our restless heart leads us to seek God and nothing other than God. "Feel your heart restless with desire for him, then do not seek anything else, because he himself is enough for you."[113] In the end, God alone satisfies the heart. "Ask for nothing else; be satisfied with that single one, for that one will satisfy you. *To you my heart has spoken: I have sought your face, O Lord, for your face will I seek.*"[114] Although our desire for God cannot be fully satisfied until we reach our heavenly homeland, we

107. Augustine, *Exposition of Psalm* 26[2].15.

108. Augustine, *Exposition of Psalm* 18.15.

109. Augustine, *Exposition of Psalm* 30[4].8.

110. Augustine, *Exposition of Psalm* 4.8.

111. Augustine, *Sermon* 34.5.

112. Augustine, *Exposition of Psalm* 26[2].23.

113. Augustine, *Exposition of Psalm* 55.17.

114. Augustine, *Exposition of Psalm* 26[2].16.

can start to possess God by loving him with our heart during our earthly journey.

Loving God with the heart also means loving the source of all virtue. Our own virtue does not bring happiness; only God, who inspires us to virtue, can make us happy. "It is not precisely your virtuous mind that makes you happy, but the one who has given you virtue, who has inspired you to desire it, and granted you the capacity for it."[115] God examines the heart and offers help so that we can delight in God and not in any other objects of delight. "So it is that the God who examines the heart and inward parts, and who identifies in the heart right thoughts and in the inward parts no inappropriate objects of delight, offers righteous help to the upright in heart, where heavenly delights are wedded to pure thoughts."[116] Being upright in heart means to take delight in heavenly things.

To be sure, when Augustine speaks of interior heavenly delights, he is not thereby discounting external action. Progress on our spiritual journey is not merely an interior act, for it inevitably leads to virtuous action. "This walking is not done by bodily feet, but by the longings of the mind and the actions of one's life."[117] The way to God is through a righteous life, for good intentions should result in good words and deeds. "The better path to God is that by which a good man hastens by the intention of his heart and mind to go by pious, just, sincere, chaste, and true words and deeds, without any wavering caused by the changing times."[118] The apostle Paul is an example of a wayfarer who had not yet reached the end of the journey but continued to grow in righteousness by being renewed inwardly day by day.[119] Such interior renewal yields righteous actions, for true progress on the journey is accomplished by living righteously and avoiding sin.[120] The righteousness of those who live by faith means "that we now move by the correctness and

115. Augustine, *Sermon* 150.9.

116. Augustine, *Exposition of Psalm* 7.11.

117. Augustine, *Punishment and Forgiveness* 2.13.20.

118. Augustine, *Letter* 234.2.

119. Augustine, *Punishment and Forgiveness* 2.13.20.

120. Augustine, *Spirit and the Letter* 36.65.

perfection of our life toward that perfection and fullness of righteousness in which love will be full and perfect in the vision of his beauty."[121] Those who live righteously by faith practice asceticism, give alms, forgive others, and persist in prayer, doing all of these things "with sound doctrine, which builds up correct faith, solid hope, and pure love."[122] The righteous become more like God, the "one, universal, incomprehensible, indefatigable, ineffable creator" by living a life of charity.[123]

According to Augustine, loving God with the heart means to be conformed to the God who is love. In Augustine's view, human beings become what they love. Our hearts are shaped by what we love. If we love material possessions, we will resemble those things. Conversely, loving God transforms us to reflect his nature. This change is profound, as loving God involves reconfiguring our inner desires to cling to him. Loving God with all our heart means loving him through his own love, a gift that changes us into his likeness. The more that we practice charity, the more that we participate in the divine life of love. Additionally, to love creatures properly, we must first love God. Only then can we truly love others and the entire created world rightly.[124]

LOVING GOD AND NEIGHBOR

Returning to the idea of love as a kind of weight, Augustine states that the weight of charity draws us toward God and others in friendship. By loving our neighbor as a spiritual creature made by God, we aim for their highest good, which is to cling to God in love. When we love another for God's sake, we are guiding them to God. In Augustine's view, this is the highest form of friendship. "Let people start loving God, and the only thing they will love

121. Augustine, *Perfection of Human Righteousness* 8.18.

122. Augustine, *Perfection of Human Righteousness* 8.18.

123. Augustine, *Letter* 234.2.

124. Augustine, *Homilies on First Epistle of John* 2.14.

in other human beings is God."[125] Since God is love, God is the source of union and communion between human beings. "What else? Ought there not to be a bond of love among human beings themselves? Indeed, there ought to be to the point that we believe that there can be no more certain step toward the love of God than the love of one human being for another."[126] By truly loving our neighbor, we grow deeper in our love for God; and by loving God with our heart, we grow in our love for our neighbor.

To be sure, for Augustine, loving God does not mean failing to love one's neighbor; rather, it means to love one's neighbor properly. For if we are to love our neighbor truly, we will bring them to love God since God is the highest good for our neighbor. This is true love. "You should do for your neighbor, then, what you do for yourself. That is, you should bring him to love God with a perfect love. For you do not love him as yourself if you do not bring him to that good toward which you yourself are striving."[127] Loving other creatures means loving them to God, in whom they find true happiness.

Loving others to help them love God means loving them for God's sake. By doing this, we set out on the journey of loving God with our whole heart. "By loving your neighbor and taking care of your neighbor, you are setting out on a journey. Where are you heading for but toward the Lord God, the one whom we should be loving with the whole heart, with the whole soul, and with the whole mind?"[128] We progress on our spiritual journey by running with charity, for all draw near to God "by following him with their faith, longing for him with their hearts, and running to him with their charity. Your feet are your charity. . . . Run toward God on these feet, draw near to him, for he himself has incited you

125. Augustine, *Sermon* 385.3.

126. Augustine, *Catholic and Manichean Way* 1.26.48.

127. Augustine, *Catholic and Manichean Way* 1.26.49.

128. Augustine, *Homilies on Gospel of John* 17.9.

to run."[129] God's love enables us to love him and to love others to God, for true charity leads us to love in the proper order.[130]

If we love God with our whole heart, we will also learn how to love ourselves properly. According to Augustine, loving God first enables us to love ourselves and our neighbors with the charity that comes from God. By truly loving God, we also learn how to love ourselves genuinely. Love of God means genuine love for ourselves since God is our highest good. If we want to love ourselves, then we should love God as our highest good. "For it is impossible that someone who loves God should fail to love himself; on the contrary, only a person who loves God knows how to love himself. After all, he loves himself sufficiently who takes care to act so that he may enjoy the highest and true good, and if that is nothing other than God, as what has already been said has taught us, who can doubt that a person who is a lover of God loves himself?"[131] Proper self-love, according to Augustine, can be found only by loving God. "Do you want to love yourself? Love God with the whole of yourself; there, you see, you will find yourself, or else in yourself you might lose yourself. If you love yourself in yourself, you are bound to fall away even from yourself, and go looking for many things besides yourself."[132]

Now that one's self-love is rooted in the love of God, one can love one's neighbor properly. "So this is your love, or love of yourself, that is, the love you love yourself with: to love God. Now I can also entrust your neighbor to you, whom you are to love as yourself."[133] By loving God with our whole heart, we can also love ourselves and our neighbors for God's sake, that is, with God as our final end and shared happiness. The love of God leads us to proper self-love and love of neighbor, for loving God requires loving God's creatures. "We must above all maintain that no one should think that he will come to happiness and to the God he loves if he holds

129. Augustine, *Exposition of Psalm* 33[2].10.

130. Augustine, *Sermon* 65A.8.

131. Augustine, *Catholic and Manichean Way* 1.26.48.

132. Augustine, *Sermon* 179A.4.

133. Augustine, *Sermon* 179A.4.

his neighbor in contempt."[134] By loving God, therefore, we learn to love creatures as God does, that is, without clinging to them as our ultimate good. The spiritual life means loving God above all things so that we might learn to love God, ourselves, and our neighbors.

Augustine understands our growth in virtue and holiness as a participation in the communal life of the church. By being a member of a community bound together in charity and celebrating the sacraments, we make progress on our journey toward God, our true happiness. "This is the Christian religion, that the one God, not many gods, be worshiped, because only the one God can make the soul happy. Participation in God makes the soul happy."[135] The way to happiness in this life is by participation in the communal life of the church. This means participation in Christian practices, including liturgical prayer, reconciliation, and works of mercy. For if we wish to be truly happy by loving God, we must also love our neighbor.

If we love others properly, we are closely knit to them, even if we are separated on the journey. "It often happens that someone who is on a journey, and far away from you, is closely knit to you because he or she loves the same things as you do. . . . But it also happens that someone close beside you is very distant from you, because he or she loves the world, whereas you love God."[136] While we may be separated from others during this life because of physical distance or even death, we remain united by a shared love of God. It is only in heaven, at the end of our earthly journey, that the happy life is perfectly fulfilled.

HEAVEN AND THE HAPPY LIFE

According to Augustine, although we can start to experience happiness in this life by loving and trusting God, the truly happy life is eternal life, which cannot be fully realized in our current

134. Augustine, *Catholic and Manichean Way* 1.26.51.

135. Augustine, *Homilies on Gospel of John* 23.5.

136. Augustine, *Exposition of Psalm* 55.2.

condition. "So that life spent in torments is not life . . . nor can it be blessed or happy, unless it's eternal."[137] The happy life is the life of blessedness with God. By living well in this life, one can reach the eternal enjoyment of God. For "only when a man who is faithful and good in these unhappy conditions passes from this life to the happy life will there really and truly be what now cannot possibly be, namely that a man lives as he would."[138] Only in heaven will we find our greatest good in God, and only in heaven will our desires be perfected. "Whatever he loves will be there, and he will not desire anything that is not there. Everything that is there will be good, and the most high God will be the most high good, and will be available for the enjoyment of his lovers, and thus total happiness will be forever assured."[139] The eternal life of heaven is the fullness of the blessed life.

In the blessedness of eternal life, we will possess God and be possessed by God. "Our happiness, then, will consist in possessing God. How should we understand this? We shall possess him, yes; but will he not also possess us? Certainly he will . . . God both possesses and is possessed, and all this is for our benefit. . . . He possesses us, and he is possessed by us, to no end other than our happiness."[140] Although our ultimate happiness cannot be fully realized in this life, we can begin to experience happiness and draw closer to God by worshiping him. "We possess him, and he possesses us, because we pay cult to him and he cultivates us."[141] Final happiness and beatitude are the rewards found in the next life, yet happiness begins in this life by growth in virtue, which is made possible by the grace of God.

> With these virtues given by God we now live a good life, and afterwards we will be given its reward, the happy life, which can only be eternal life. For the same virtues are

137. Augustine, *Sermon* 306.6.
138. Augustine, *Trinity* 13.7.10.
139. Augustine, *Trinity* 13.7.10.
140. Augustine, *Exposition of Psalm* 32[3].18.
141. Augustine, *Exposition of Psalm* 32[3].18.

> practiced here and will have their result there. . . . And so all good and holy people, even amid torments of every sort, supported by God's help, are called happy because of the hope for that end, the end in which they will be happy.[142]

Growth in virtue enables us to make progress along the journey to our heavenly homeland, where we will find our true and lasting happiness. The end of our journey is Christ. When we arrive at him, we will arrive at our final end.

> Now Christ is the end of all our striving, because however hard we try, we are made perfect only in him and by him. Our perfection is to reach him. But when you reach him you will look for nothing further, for he is your end . . . when you reach him, you will desire nothing further, because you could never have anything better. Christ has set us an example of how to live our lives here, and he will give us our reward in the life to come.[143]

During this life, if we open our heart to God, Christ will begin to dwell in us so that we can attain to the glory of heaven.[144] Returning to the heart means returning to the Lord, since Christ's image can be found in the interior human being. "Return to the heart; see there what perhaps you may sense about God, because that is where God's image is. Christ is dwelling in the inner self; in the inner self you are being renewed after the image of God."[145] Our renewal begins in this life and is perfected in the next, when our striving will cease and we will behold God in heaven.[146]

According to Augustine, our true home country is heaven. We ought to hunger and thirst for our homeland while we are travelers on our journey. "We are hungry and thirsty, you see, provided, that is, we acknowledge ourselves to be travelers. Those who

142. Augustine, *Letter* 155.4.16.

143. Augustine, *Exposition of Psalm* 56.2.

144. Augustine, *Homilies on First Epistle of John* 8.1.

145. Augustine, *Homilies on Gospel of John* 18.10.

146. Augustine, *Letter* 148.2.8.

are traveling, and know they are traveling, long to reach home; and because they are longing for home, they find the traveling irksome."[147] Sometimes we can forget our home, especially if we cling to the things of this world. Yet Christ dwells in the hearts of those who have faith and love him. "Rightly, then, will the hearts of those who are satisfied live for age upon age. For their life is Christ, who dwells in their hearts, now through faith but afterwards through vision."[148] For those who examine their hearts and cultivate the desire for God, Christ will dwell in their hearts in faith until they arrive at their heavenly homeland.

CONCLUSION

Augustine offers spiritual guidance to all in search of true and lasting happiness. According to Augustine, the entire spiritual life is an exercise of the heart's desire. If we turn within and examine our heart, we will find that our deepest desire is for God. Since we are created by God and for God, we can discover true happiness only in God. But how can we come to know God in this life? Because God is truth, beauty, and goodness, Augustine teaches that by seeking the truth, we can begin our journey to the God who is truth. Similarly, by gazing upon the beautiful things in creation, we will be led to contemplate the creator of all that is beautiful. Ultimately, by striving to possess the good, we can come to possess God and be possessed by him. Only God can satisfy the human heart. Loving God with all our heart teaches us how to love ourselves, our neighbors, and all of creation properly, with God as our ultimate goal and true happiness.

In the following chapter, we will examine Augustine's view of God as creator. Why did God create, and what is the relationship between God and his creation? Additionally, we will look at how spiritual beings turned away from God and now live in exile. We all originate from God, but because of our misuse of freedom, we

147. Augustine, *Sermon* 378.1.

148. Augustine, *Letter* 140.25.62.

are far from God, searching for our way home. Augustine's teachings on creation and the fall help us understand where we start on our spiritual journey and how we can begin to find our way back to our heavenly homeland.

2

The Journey from God

Creation and Fall

But if one asks about God's reason for creating, no quicker or better reason is given in reply than that every creature of God is good. And what is more worthy of the good God than that he should make good things that no one can make but God?

—Augustine, *Letter* 166.5.15

IN THE YEAR 415, Augustine wrote a letter to Jerome, a renowned priest and Scripture scholar, regarding the origin of the soul, creation, and sin. In the letter, Augustine addresses some of the complex issues surrounding these topics and acknowledges that many of them cannot be resolved. However, what can be said of the soul is that it is good, immortal, and not a part of God.[1] Every creature made by God is good, for God is a good creator.[2] Furthermore, the soul has not fallen into sin because of God, but rather because of the soul's misuse of free will.[3] Every spiritual creature needs

1. Augustine, *Letter* 166.3.5.
2. Augustine, *Letter* 166.5.15.
3. Augustine, *Letter* 166.3.5.

the grace of Christ, the mediator between God and humanity, to be redeemed.[4]

Augustine's letter to Jerome summarizes his view of creation and original sin. The main point of Augustine's argument is that God is a good creator. Everything God creates is good. This is crucial for Christian spirituality because all spiritual beings come from the good God and will return to the good God. But if everything God creates is good, then where does sin come from?

In this chapter, we will examine the key features of Augustine's teaching on creation to understand what it means to be spiritual beings made by a good God. Augustine's evolving view of creation from nothing, or *creatio ex nihilo*, demonstrates creation's complete dependence on God. Not only did God create the universe in the beginning, but God also continues to sustain creation at every moment. Creation results from God's ongoing action and goodness. God desires that we share in the goodness of God's own being. Next, we will explore the creation of humanity in God's image, a teaching that has significant implications for human dignity. Finally, we will look at the origin of sin and how spiritual beings have turned away from their creator, leading to a fallen and broken world. Only through God's grace can spiritual beings find healing and begin their journey back to God.

THE MEANING OF CREATION

Why do we exist? What is the meaning or purpose behind our existence? Why is there something instead of nothing? These fundamental questions of philosophy and theology were central to Augustine's thoughts. Although we might not have the same academic background in philosophy and theology as Augustine, we are all philosophers in our own right. That is, we all face certain unavoidable questions about the meaning of our lives. Since we did not create ourselves, to what or to whom are we indebted for

4. Augustine, *Letter* 166.3.5.

our existence? Where do we come from? What is the purpose of our being?

One way to address such questions is to argue that our existence has no inherent meaning. This perspective appears in both ancient and contemporary philosophical and religious traditions. It suggests that our existence arises from chance, with the universe itself being the result of random, chaotic forces. We are merely products of molecular reactions within the material world. However, this raises a fundamental question: From where does matter originate? What is the ultimate source of our universe?

Augustine offers a compelling argument that we owe our existence to God, who created us for a noble purpose. The reason for our existence is to participate in God's own goodness. The core meaning of creation is to receive the gift of being. Our very existence is a share in God's goodness. However, within the doctrine of creation, there are other questions to explore. For example, how did God create? What is God's relationship to creation? In what sense is God the cause of creation? Is creation a one-time event or an ongoing process? Augustine addresses all of these questions in his nuanced teaching on creation.

After Augustine rejected Manicheism, his view of creation was heavily influenced by Platonic philosophy. From the Platonists, Augustine gained a metaphysical foundation for the existence of the universe. According to the Platonic tradition, the entire universe as we know it finds its ultimate source and origin in God, also called the One. All things come from the One and will return to the One. God is the cause of existence and the creator of souls.[5]

In Platonic philosophy, the reason for creation is the overflowing of goodness, which flows from the One. Creation is seen as an emanation from the One, the origin of everything that exists. This creates a hierarchy of existence, with God or the One at the highest point. All other beings, including spiritual ones, derive from the One. Angels possess spiritual bodies that need no nourishment and surpass material bodies,[6] and they sit at the highest

5. Augustine, *City of God* 8.5.

6. Augustine, *Literal Meaning of Genesis* 6.19.30.

level of creatures within the hierarchy.[7] Next are human beings, who have spiritual souls and material bodies, followed by animals, plants, and inanimate matter.[8] According to the Platonic hierarchy of being, everything that exists comes from the same source, namely, the One or God.

Augustine adopted the Platonic hierarchy of being, yet he also modified it. He made a significant change to the doctrine of creation based on his reading of Scripture. Creation is not the result of an impersonal emanation or diffusion of goodness from the One. This would make God passive and a bystander as creation unfolds. Conversely, in Augustine's view, creation is an activity of God. God wills that all things exist in their proper order. Based on his reading of Genesis, Augustine argues that God freely chooses to create things and to declare them good. Therefore, although he uses the framework of the Platonic hierarchy of being, Augustine insists that God actively wills the creation of the universe. The reason for creation is not a passive overflow or emanation of goodness. Instead, the reason for creation is God's active will to create all things good.

Augustine interprets the creation stories in Genesis to suggest that God freely chooses to create and declare everything good. The reason behind creation is a good God.[9] Creation exists to share in God's goodness. God chooses to create things that partake in his own goodness and being. There is no hidden agenda behind creation. We are not here to be manipulated by a higher power for sinister purposes, nor must we live in constant suspicion of the creator's motives. Instead, the only reason for creation is God's own goodness, which he desires to share with the entire created universe. As Augustine states, the good God created all things good, and even philosophers like Plato concluded that a good God

7. Augustine, *City of God* 12.2.

8. Augustine, *City of God* 11.16.

9. Augustine, *City of God* 11.21.

is the reason for a good world.[10] The entire reason for creation is so that the "good God might create good things."[11]

Another implication of Augustine's teaching is that creation is completely gratuitous. There was no benefit for God in creating the world. God does not gain anything from creation; instead, creation benefits by receiving the unmerited gift of existence. God creates out of pure gratuitous goodness, for as Augustine states, "Solely by your abundant goodness has your creation come to be and stood firm, for you did not want so good a thing to be missing. It could be of no profit to you."[12] God creates the universe so that creatures might come to share in the goodness of his life. "What are we to say to him who in the beginning made us absolutely *gratis*, simply because he is good, and not because we deserved anything?"[13] Our existence is an unmerited gift.

Furthermore, the Genesis stories show that everything is good because of God's goodness. "As I contemplated your works, what I saw was this: that there can be nothing good in us, unless it comes from you who made us."[14] Some things are better than others,[15] not because some things are intrinsically evil, but rather because of their position in the hierarchy of being. Some beings have intellect and will, allowing them to know and love God. These spiritual beings include angels and humans, who can understand God and love him. Therefore, spiritual beings are ranked higher in the hierarchy of creation than animals, plants, and inanimate objects. However, all created things are considered good because they originate from the good God.

Christian revelation goes beyond Platonic philosophy by asserting that the divine reason for creation is love. God is love, and God freely created spiritual beings so they could share in God's divine life of love. Citing 1 John 4:16, Augustine states that "God

10. Augustine, *City of God* 11.21.
11. Augustine, *City of God* 11.22.
12. Augustine, *Confessions* 13.2.2.
13. Augustine, *Exposition of Psalm* 43.15.
14. Augustine, *Exposition of Psalm* 142.10.
15. Augustine, *City of God* 11.22.

is love, and he who abides in love, it says, abides in God and God abides in him. . . . Let God be your dwelling, and let your dwelling be God's."[16] Spiritual creatures find their home in God, who created all things out of love.

Augustine's doctrine of creation centers on his view of God as the beginning and end of everything. As transcendent truth, beauty, and goodness, God makes the created world good and beautiful. He is the origin of all measure, form, and order.[17] Creation naturally moves toward God as its ultimate good, and its temporary nature shows its development toward beauty and order through God's providence.[18] God created all things, including time itself, in order for created things to become truly happy.[19] The triune God is the creator of everything and the one in whom all spiritual beings find true happiness. "The supreme and true God, therefore, with his Word and his Spirit, which three are one, is the one almighty God, the creator and maker of every soul and every body. It is by participation in him that all are happy who are happy in truth and not in empty illusion."[20] God created the world so that spiritual beings could come to know his truth, goodness, and love.[21]

God's providential care operates through his creative activity. For Augustine, God is not just one cause among many; rather, God is a transcendent or primary cause whose actions do not conflict with creaturely causality. Since God transcends creation, he can care for all creatures and provide what is necessary for spiritual beings to find their way home, for "there is not one among these creatures that he did not make, and he takes care of them all."[22] This perspective on divine providence bears significance not only for spirituality but also for modern science. Based on an Augustinian doctrine of creation, there is no conflict between Christian

16. Augustine, *Homilies on First Epistle of John* 9.1.

17. Augustine, *City of God* 11.15.

18. Augustine, *Literal Meaning of Genesis* 6.15.26.

19. Augustine, *City of God* 11.4.

20. Augustine, *City of God* 5.11.

21. Augustine, *Exposition of Psalm* 145.13.

22. Augustine, *Exposition of Psalm* 145.13.

theology and the natural sciences. God has created a universe with a natural order, yet because God is a transcendent cause, God remains active and present throughout all of creation.

Following the Christian tradition that came before him, Augustine affirms the doctrine of *creatio ex nihilo*, or creation from nothing. This teaching is based on the idea that God is the ultimate cause of everything, but God's causality goes beyond the created order. God's creative activity is ongoing, and creation relies on God at every moment for its existence. God did not create the world from some preexisting eternal matter but instead from nothing, which shows creation's contingency or total dependence on God.

CREATION FROM NOTHING

Augustine's claim that God created from nothing affirms God's immutability, meaning God's unchanging nature, whereas creatures are subject to change. "Hence, I ask you what the universe of creatures was made out of. Although it is good in its own kind, it is still inferior to the creator and mutable, while the creator remains immutable, and you will not find anything to answer unless you admit that it was made of nothing."[23] God alone is the almighty and unchanging source of all that exists, for there is absolutely no nature which he did not create.[24] Creation is completely dependent upon God for its existence, whereas God does not depend on creation in any way. Thus, there is a kind of asymmetry between creator and creation, for God does not change, while creatures are constantly in a process of transformation.

Does this asymmetry imply that God is somehow cold or distant from creation? In fact, because God is the transcendent cause of everything, God can be present throughout all creation in a way no other being can. Additionally, the doctrine of *creatio ex nihilo* highlights the absolute contingency of creation, emphasizing God's free and voluntary choice to create so that all may partake

23. Augustine, *Answer to Secundus* 8.

24. Augustine, *Sermon* 214.2.

in his goodness. God is not forced to create; instead, God's will freely brings creation into existence. Moreover, God continuously sustains all creatures in being. This ongoing act of creation shows God's love for creation.

Augustine explains that from the divine perspective, God created all things at the same time. However, from a creaturely perspective, some things are created at different times for specific purposes.[25] "So this God, then, living in unchanging eternity, created all things simultaneously. . . . Some of these things he created were spiritual, some corporeal."[26] Since the creator God is the triune God, all things exist in the Word, according to God's plan.[27] God created spiritual beings so that they might come to know and love him, while corporeal things demonstrate God's goodness and beauty.[28] As the Scriptures reveal, God spoke all things into being, which further illustrates the contingency of creation.[29] For nothing would exist if God did not will to create and sustain the universe in being.

The opening verse of the book of Genesis shows how God is the source of creation. Only God is eternal, infinite, and unchanging, so matter is not eternal. The creation stories in Genesis depict God's voluntary decision to create all things by declaring, "Let it be made."[30] Augustine interprets the creation stories in Genesis using a figurative approach. Genesis is a book about God's creative work and his relationship with creation. It is not a scientific textbook or a historical record. Instead, it aims to tell stories that convey deeper theological truths. Genesis shows that God is the transcendent source of both material and spiritual realities.

As Scripture reveals, God creates both spiritual and material beings. The angels are rational, spiritual creatures with spiritual bodies, whereas human beings have spiritual souls and material

25. Augustine, *Confessions* 11.7.9.

26. Augustine, *Literal Meaning of Genesis* 8.20.39.

27. Augustine, *Exposition of Psalm* 44.5.

28. Augustine, *Confessions* 13.2.2.

29. Augustine, *Confessions* 11.7.9.

30. Augustine, *Literal Meaning of Genesis* 1.4.9.

bodies. Augustine interprets the creation of light on the first day as a figure of God's creation of the angels.[31] "Day" in this creation narrative does not refer to a twenty-four-hour period because the sun and moon are not created until the fourth day.[32] "Day" has a deeper spiritual meaning in relation to God's ongoing creative activity. God creates the angels on the first day, for they are members of the heavenly city of God.[33] The angels are creatures with intellect and will, and they were created to love and contemplate God as the Highest Being.[34] Angels are spiritual creatures signified by the light for they resemble God, yet they remain distinct from God.[35]

Human beings, like angels, are rational creatures with intellect and will, yet they also possess material bodies. Moreover, Gen 1:26–27 reveals that human beings are created in the image and likeness of God, which is essential to understanding humanity's unique dignity as a spiritual creature. Let us turn now to Augustine's understanding of humanity as the image of God.

CREATED IN THE IMAGE OF GOD

In Augustine's theology, human beings possess special dignity as creatures made in God's image and likeness. As the image of God, human beings bear the imprint of the good God.[36] The entire created world is good and beautiful because it has been made by the good God, but God has made human beings in his image and likeness so that they might come to know him and cling to him in love. "Observe the beauty of the world, and praise the plan of the creator. Observe what he has made, love the one who made it. Hold on to this maxim above all: love the one who made it, because he also made you, his lover, in his own image."[37] Human beings are

31. Augustine, *Literal Meaning of Genesis* 5.19.37.
32. Augustine, *Literal Meaning of Genesis* 5.2.4.
33. Augustine, *Literal Meaning of Genesis* 5.19.37.
34. Augustine, *City of God* 12.6.
35. Augustine, *Answer to an Enemy* 1.7.10.
36. Augustine, *City of God* 11.28.
37. Augustine, *Sermon* 68.5.

made for loving union and communion with God. Since we bear the image of God, we are meant to be in a loving relationship with him.

According to Augustine, being God's "lover" means entering into a loving relationship with the creator. This intimate relationship is realized and perfected through the union of Christ and the church. The church is meant to be one body with Christ, symbolized by the union of man and woman (Eph 5:31–32). From the beginning, God's plan has been to invite humanity into a unique relationship with him. Matrimony is a sign that points to the relationship between creator and creature. Human beings find the fulfillment of their deepest desire by entering into loving union and communion with God. With spiritual souls made in God's image, humans can know God as their true love.

The Christian doctrine of *creatio ex nihilo* shows that the spiritual soul is created for union with God in love. Following the tradition before him, Augustine asserts that the human soul was made from nothing and is not some preexisting eternal matter.[38] This points to the fact that the soul is uniquely made in God's image, not the image of some previous material thing. For Augustine, the soul is the primary image of God precisely because it is capable of knowing and loving the creator. This does not mean that the body is evil or just an addition to human nature; as we have seen, God creates everything good, including material bodies. The human body is formed from the earth, but the soul is not made from any prior matter, since it is created in the image of God, who is Spirit. "It was out of nothing that God made the soul which he gave to the first man, not out of some creature already made, like the body out of earth; and that is why when it goes back it has nowhere to go back to except the author who gave it, not to any creature it was made out of, like the body to earth."[39] The spiritual soul comes from God and will return to God.

Since humanity is both spiritual and material, humanity is a microcosm of all creation, for "all creation is also present in a

38. Augustine, *Literal Meaning of Genesis* 10.9.16.

39. Augustine, *Literal Meaning of Genesis* 10.9.16.

human being . . . all creation is partly invisible and partly visible."[40] Human beings consist of both invisible spiritual souls and visible material bodies according to God's creative plan. God is the source of life for spiritual souls. "He himself, then, made not just the one breath that he breathed into the first man, who was made from the earth, but every breath, and he himself still makes every breath."[41] The body is good since God created all material things good, for "how can the body be evil, when even the souls are advised to imitate the harmony of its members?"[42] Souls imitate the unity and harmony of the body, yet such harmony can be bestowed upon souls only by God. The human being united with God serves as an image of the unity and harmony of all creation.

Furthermore, God has created humanity in his image so that God can dwell in the human heart. God makes his dwelling in the heart as "the human soul draws near," because "in that image it was created from the first."[43] Because human beings are created in God's image, they are endowed with special dignity. All people, from the first parents to their descendants, are inherently worthy of union with God. Since all humans are designed for loving communion with God, they possess a unique dignity that belongs to creatures with a supernatural destiny.

Augustine acknowledges that angels, like human beings, are spiritual creatures with reason and intellect, and therefore, they are also made in God's image and likeness. However, if God has created all things good and God is supremely wise and good,[44] how did sin enter the world? What is the origin of sin and evil? While Augustine acknowledges that the ultimate origin of iniquity is a mystery, he nevertheless appeals to scriptural narratives to illustrate how angels and humans have fallen away from God through the misuse of the gift of freedom.

40. Augustine, *Answer to Secundus* 8.

41. Augustine, *Letter* 190.5.16.

42. Augustine, *Continence* 10.24.

43. Augustine, *Exposition of Psalm* 99.5.

44. Augustine, *City of God* 11.28.

FALLING AWAY FROM GOD

According to Augustine, Scripture reveals that human beings and some angels used their freedom to turn away from God.[45] The consequence of having rejected God is felt throughout all of creation. The world we encounter on a daily basis is broken, fallen, and fragile. Our experience in this life is filled with chaos, disorder, and corruption. This happens because some of God's free spiritual creatures—namely, angels and human beings—misused their freedom. If God created angels and humans good by nature, then how and why would these good creatures turn away from God?

The origin of sin is mysterious, yet Augustine turns to the biblical notion of pride as the root and cause of all sin. "Pride is the beginning of all sin . . . we also read, 'The beginning of a man's pride is to fall away from God' (Sir 10:14)."[46] Pride, or in Latin *superbia*, is the first of the vices, and it is what led some angels to reject God. Likewise, *superbia* is at the root of the first parents' disobedience of God in the garden of Eden.[47] As we have seen, pride in its essence is the desire to replace God with oneself. It is a form of self-sufficiency that looks to oneself as the arbiter of truth and the source of delight, and thereby as the ultimate good.[48] Pride is a rejection of God as the one true and immutable good to which a spiritual creature must cling in order to be happy.[49]

Pride is a denial of the need for God. It is a rejection of one's creaturely nature, and it is an attempt to usurp the creator's place in the hierarchy of being. By seeking to take the place of God, the creature is destined for unhappiness, for only God is the source of a spiritual creature's true happiness.[50] Pride is, in effect, a disordered self-love, for it is the desire to cling to one's own truth and

45. Augustine, *City of God* 11.11.
46. Augustine, *Letter* 140.28.68.
47. Augustine, *Sermon* 340A.1; *Sermon* 346B.3; 354.5; *City of God* 12.6.
48. Augustine, *City of God* 14.13.
49. Augustine, *City of God* 12.1.
50. Augustine, *City of God* 12.1.

goodness apart from God. In Augustine's view, this kind of pride can lead only to misery.

Why would any rational creature turn away from God, the source of our true and lasting happiness? Could this be attributed to a defect in the creature? Augustine argues that the fall cannot be due to a defective nature, for all creatures are created good. Rather, the fall is the result of the misuse of good will. Evil is not a created thing but an absence or perversion of an intended good. "Evil is not a nature of any kind, but the loss of the good has been given this name."[51] Pride is an abuse of the will, or what Augustine calls "a harmful freedom," as a kind of insubordination and perverse imitation of God.[52] Augustine concludes that there is no efficient cause for the turning of the will from good to evil. Instead, one can speak only of a deficient cause whereby a rational creature would turn away from God, who is goodness itself.[53] For Augustine, there is no good reason for a rational creature to turn away from God, for evil is by definition a defect or absence of good. Thus, sin is irrational. It can be described, but it cannot be explained sufficiently, for there is no good reason for a good creature to turn away from God, who is the source of goodness.

THE TWO CITIES

The falling away of Lucifer or Satan and the rebellious angels led to the founding of a body of spiritual creatures separated from God. This was the beginning of the "earthly" or "wicked city," which is set against the heavenly city.[54] These two cities are separated by their loves, the former by the love of self "even to the point of contempt for God," and the latter by the love of God, "even to the

51. Augustine, *Literal Meaning of Genesis* 8.14.31.
52. Augustine, *Literal Meaning of Genesis* 8.14.31.
53. Augustine, *City of God* 12.7.
54. Augustine, *City of God* 11.1, 11.11–19; 14.28.

point of contempt for self."[55] The world in its current condition is marked by the intermingling of these two cities.

In Augustine's view, the two cities are composed of both angels and human beings. The wicked earthly city consists of the proud, who seek their own ends and whose king is the devil. The city of God, on the other hand, consists of the humble, whose king is Christ.[56] The difficulty is that there are citizens of both cities in all communities in this world.

The fall of the first human beings, Adam and Eve, described in the book of Genesis affects all human beings.[57] All are born in a fallen state and begin as citizens of the earthly city, in "captivity to sin."[58] Only by God's grace can human beings be transformed in order to become members of the heavenly city of God. The figure of Abel, the first righteous man after the fall of Adam and Eve, represents the members of the heavenly city, whereas Cain represents the earthly city.[59] The two cities will be separated by God definitively at the eschaton or end-time, but until then, they are intermingled while on journey toward their final ends.[60] During this time, good and wicked citizens are mixed, such that only God knows who will constitute the two cities in the end.[61]

THE EFFECTS OF THE FALL

Why did Adam and Eve's act of disobedience affect all of humanity? In Augustine's view, the answer lies in the profound rupture of the harmony that creation had initially enjoyed. There are three primary effects of the fall of Adam and Eve. First, there is a vitiation or weakening of the human will. As Augustine puts it, the punishment for the first parents' disobedience was disobedience

55. Augustine, *City of God* 14.28.
56. Augustine, *Exposition of Psalm* 61.6.
57. Augustine, *Literal Meaning of Genesis* 8.13.28–30; *City of God* 14.11.
58. Augustine, *Exposition of Psalm* 136.1.
59. Augustine, *Exposition of Psalm* 61.6; 64.2; *City of God* 15.1–8.
60. Augustine, *Exposition of Psalm* 51.4; 36[1].12.
61. Augustine, *Exposition of Psalm* 61.8; 64.2.

itself. This explains the experience of the mixed desires of the human heart and the apparent battle between the spirit and the flesh, for "our own flesh, which was once subject to us, now brings us distress by not serving us, although we, by not serving God, are only able to bring distress upon ourselves."[62] Matter, per se, is not the reason for the struggle between the soul and the body; instead, the struggle of desires in the fallen state of the material world is due to the sickness of pride. "Besides, the so-called pains of the flesh are actually pains of the soul which are experienced in the flesh and from the flesh."[63] The material body is no longer under the perfect control of the soul.[64] The effects of the fall are felt in terms of the soul and the body, such that the body has become "fleshly" and at odds with the soul. The human being is now at war, as experienced by the disordered desires of the heart and the struggle between body and soul.

Second, as a result of having freely rejected God, who is the source of life, human beings now experience death of the body and of the spirit. "By his own will, he was dead in spirit, and, against his own will, he was going to die in body as well."[65] The separation of body and soul is called the first death, but the second death is spiritual separation from God. Humanity rejected eternal life and would fall into eternal death, unless saved by grace. Augustine's point is that the rejection of God led to a corruption of the communion between God and humanity. This corruption introduced bodily and spiritual death to human beings who would have otherwise remained "in the enjoyment of God," for in paradise, "true gladness flowed continually from God," and "between husband and wife there was a faithful partnership of genuine love, an alertness of mind and body in true concord, and an effortless observance of the commandment."[66] As a result of the fall, corruption

62. Augustine, *City of God* 14.15.

63. Augustine, *City of God* 14.15.

64. Augustine, *City of God* 14.5.

65. Augustine, *City of God* 14.15.

66. Augustine, *City of God* 14.26.

and decay entered into humanity's original concord, and human beings are now cut off from God and eternal life.

Third, the fall had devastating effects on human society and on creation as a whole. As a consequence of the fall, human beings not only experience conflict within themselves, they also experience division and corruption in their relationships with others. This was revealed with the introduction of lust into paradise. Adam and Eve no longer enjoyed perfect blessedness and harmony. Instead of living in concord, harmony, and trust, human beings now live in discord, enmity, and suspicion. Thus, as a result of the fall of Adam and Eve, there are three primary consequences: (1) corruption of the union between body and soul; (2) the separation of body and soul or death, and separation of the soul from God; and (3) discord between human beings and disharmony in all of creation.

ORIGINAL SIN

The fall of Adam and Eve, also known as original sin, has effects on all human beings. According to Augustine, original sin is handed down through propagation. To be clear, Augustine is not suggesting that sexual intercourse is intrinsically evil. However, it is by propagation that original sin is passed on because every human being is born into a fallen, weakened condition. Prior to the fall, Augustine speculates that the first parents would have enjoyed sexuality and procreation without any hint of lust.[67] However, after the first act of disobedience, all human beings experience the lust of the flesh, whereby they are no longer in complete control of their bodily members.[68] Thus, sexuality after the fall is marked by the disobedience of the body, resulting in shame.[69] This experience of shameful lust also marks fallen human relationships, for instead of living in perfect harmony and concord, human beings in their pride now seek to dominate others. This is what Augustine

67. Augustine, *City of God* 14.21–24.

68. Augustine, *City of God* 14.16–17.

69. Augustine, *City of God* 14.23.

calls the lust for domination, or in Latin *libido dominandi*, which is characteristic of the earthly city and worldly rulers.[70] The lust for domination leads to corruption within marriage and within society. Human beings were made for union and communion, yet as a consequence of the fall, they are now dominated by lust.[71] "For there is nothing more contentious by virtue of its fault than the human race, but also nothing more social by virtue of its nature."[72] In this fallen condition, human beings are also subject to evils present in the material world such as disease, for bodily creation is no longer in harmony as God intended.[73]

In the garden of Eden, Adam and Eve enjoyed a distinctive kind of freedom, but after their free rejection of God, all human beings share in the guilt and consequences of original sin. In this fallen condition, human beings cannot will the good without God's grace. That is, after the fall of the first parents, God's grace is necessary to do any good. One key feature of Augustine's teaching on original sin is that after the fall, human beings remain in the image of God despite the corruption due to sin. Human nature is not intrinsically corrupt. Pride is the cause of corruption. The good God created human beings good, yet human beings live in a weakened state. "Catholics say that human nature was created good by the good God the creator, but that, having been wounded by sin, it needs Christ the physician."[74] Humanity remains in the image and likeness of God. The image has been deformed and corrupted, but the image cannot be completely destroyed by sin. After the fall, humanity is deeply afflicted and in need of God's healing, but this healing is possible precisely because the image of God remains in the midst of corruption. The remedy for such corruption is grace, given freely to humanity through Christ and the church. In the following chapters, we will consider how Christ

70. Augustine, *City of God* 14.28.

71. Augustine, *City of God* 1.pref.

72. Augustine, *City of God* 12.28.

73. Augustine, *City of God* 14.26; *Literal Meaning of Genesis* 8.23.44.

74. Augustine, *Marriage and Desire* 2.9.

heals wounded humanity by the gift of grace and how this grace is mediated by the church.

CONCLUSION

Augustine's understanding of creation, influenced by Platonic philosophy and his interpretation of Scripture, suggests that our existence is a gift from God's gratuitous goodness. God wills that we live, move, and have our being in him. Our journey begins with God's action to create spiritual beings who can find their way back to him. The entire created universe is good because it has its origin and sustenance from the good God. God's only motive for creating is his will for creatures to share in his goodness. Furthermore, God's creative activity is continuous, not limited to a single moment in time. God sustains us in every moment of our existence, and he is a transcendent cause beyond any cause in the created world. This means that God sustains us with the gift of our very being.

God created spiritual creatures in his image by endowing them with intellect and will, which enable them to know and love him. Each human being is bestowed with inherent dignity because each person is made in the image of God. Despite the fundamental goodness of creation, something went wrong. Spiritual creatures misused and abused their freedom, leading to their separation from God. In Christian teaching, this is commonly referred to as the fall. The consequences of this turning away from God are extensive. The fall of both angels and humans brought sin, death, and destruction into the world. Spiritual beings wandered far away from God. In this condition, creation needs healing and restoration, which only God can provide. The fall also illustrates how creation is entirely dependent on God.

This chapter explored Augustine's doctrine of creation and fall as two essential movements in our spiritual journey. We come from God as our first source, yet we exist in a fallen world marked by the effects of sin. Augustine's view of original sin, which has been formative in the Western Christian tradition, offers an explanation for our experience of death and corruption. It also draws us to contemplate our need for God's grace, which alone can bring us healing and restoration. Meditating on creation and fall can lead us to a deeper awareness of our dependence on God as spiritual creatures in search of our way home.

In the next chapter, we will consider Augustine's solution to the problem of our separation from God, namely, Christ and the church. According to the Christian tradition, God became a human being in Christ in order to heal fallen humanity.[75] For Augustine, Christ becomes the way home for fallen human beings seeking their heavenly homeland. Christ's mission of human redemption and salvation is accomplished through the church, by which the members of Christ's body are healed and united in an unbreakable bond of love.

75. Augustine, *Letter* 177.11.

3

The Way to God
Christ and the Church

Christ came mainly for this reason, that the human race might know how much God loves us, and might know this in order to glow with love for him by whom we have first been loved, and might love our neighbor according to the command and the example of him who became our neighbor.
—Augustine, *Instructing Beginners in Faith* 4.8

AROUND THE YEAR 404, Augustine wrote to a deacon in Carthage named Deogratias who had encountered some problems in pastoral ministry. Deogratias asked Augustine how to present the teachings of the Christian faith effectively to newcomers who seemed uninterested in church doctrine. He also wanted to know how to remain joyful in the face of such struggles. Augustine's reply is a two-part treatise titled *Instructing Beginners in Faith*. In this work, Augustine offers two examples of how to teach salvation history using scriptural narratives. He suggests that the key to maintaining joy in ministry is to focus on the truth that Christ died and shed his blood for the salvation of the world. For those responsible for guiding newcomers in the faith, the source of joy isn't found in eloquent speech or the number of converts but in the truth that every soul seeking to join the church is redeemed by Christ's blood and will be saved from sin and death. This truth should serve as the firm foundation of Christian faith and ministry. Furthermore, Augustine asserts that God allows the church to face scandals to refine and purify it. This does not mean God causes evil or scandal; rather, despite scandals among the members of the church, God can bring good out of the church's failures, just as he brought the greatest good from Christ's sacrifice and death on the cross.

For those seeking progress in their spiritual life, Augustine offers a clear path forward. If we forget the way back to our spiritual home, then we can turn to Christ, the incarnate God, who became the way beneath our feet to lead us home. In Christ, God became human so that we might know the depth of God's love for us and be set ablaze with love. Despite our weaknesses, Christ chose to become one of us to heal us and to provide the medicine of his humility. The humility of Christ is a healing balm for the sickness of our pride. In the end, God's love is the goal we must strive for so we can journey to our heavenly homeland. The more we grow in love for God and neighbor, the more we advance on the way to our spiritual home.

In this chapter, we will examine Augustine's Christology, or his understanding of Jesus Christ as both divine and human. As the eternal Word, Christ is equal to the Father. As a human, Christ is truly one of us. Only the God-man can provide us with healing and salvation, according to God's plan. Christ redeems fallen humanity and offers the gift of eternal life. Christ is the source of grace for the church. In Augustine's view, the whole Christ includes Christ the head and the members of his body, the church. God's plan of salvation is fulfilled in the church as the body of Christ. However, the church on earth remains in a state of pilgrimage, and the members are sinners in a process of transformation and conformation to Christ the head.

The church is truly the body of Christ, yet it is not in a state of perfection or sinlessness. All of the members of the church are sinners and must depend on God's grace and forgiveness during their journey through this world. The church on pilgrimage is in a process of purification. Meanwhile, the church should be ready to face scandal and sinfulness among its members. The church is a mixed body of good and wicked. Each person is in a weakened state and remains vulnerable to sin. This should foster greater compassion toward others since all are in need of healing. God permits the church to undergo testing and purification as a demonstration of his mercy, patience, and long-suffering. We should not be surprised to encounter scandal in the church. However, this should not lead us to despair or presumption, but rather, this can cause us to rely more on God's grace and his saving activity. God's providence is at work, and his plan will not fail. Therefore, our hope is in God, who is shaping the church as the one body of Christ united in love.

We will begin by examining how Christ acts as the mediator between God and humanity. As the God-man who is fully divine and fully human, Christ is the only one who can offer forgiveness of sins, heal fallen human nature, and invite participation in the divine life. Then, we will consider how Christ serves as the source of grace for fallen humanity, guiding us back to our heavenly homeland. Next, we will explore Augustine's rich understanding of the church as the body of Christ, which, together with Christ as the head, forms the whole Christ. The church on earth is on a journey of growth, transformation, and purification from sin. Finally, we will analyze Augustine's view of the church as the city of God on its journey toward its heavenly homeland.

CHRIST THE MEDIATOR

Like many of his foundational teachings, Augustine's Christology evolved over time and in different settings. His Christology took shape in the midst of controversies with groups such as the Manicheans, the Arians, and the Pelagians. As a bishop and spiritual leader, Augustine encouraged his congregation to place their hope and trust in God, whose salvific plan is fulfilled through Christ and the church.

Augustine's Christology developed in opposition to the views of the Manicheans, especially after his baptism and entry into the church. The Manicheans saw Jesus mainly as a teacher sent from the realm of light to impart divine knowledge. They believed the world results from a mixture of light and darkness. Salvation is a consequence of the liberation of light from the darkness of the material world. According to the Manicheans, Jesus is neither fully human nor fully divine. He can be called Son of God because he comes to earth to reveal divine knowledge, but he is not truly God. Titles such as Wisdom and Power of God show that he originates from the realm of light. Jesus is not God according to the Christian tradition that the Manicheans professed. Additionally, they believed Jesus only appeared to become human and to die on the cross. The Manicheans considered the suffering of Jesus unthinkable, since Jesus was sent from the realm of light to deliver the saving knowledge needed to free humans from the corruption of material bodies.[1]

Augustine rejected Manichean Christology because he concluded that salvation is not simply about gaining knowledge. He also dismissed the idea that human beings are principally spiritual souls that need to be freed from material bodies. Instead, he saw humans as both spirit and matter—body and soul. Salvation involves healing our entire human nature. Furthermore, salvation is not about the liberation of light to an eternal realm; rather, eternal life is a gift freely given by God. Since Jesus is fully divine and fully human, he can bestow the gift of eternal life and provide healing for our wounded human nature. This forms the core of Augustine's evolving Christology.

Augustine's understanding of Jesus as both God and human is vital to Christian spirituality, because only God can save souls made in God's own image and likeness. Christ is the one mediator between God and humanity who offers the gift of salvation. Although it is possible for God to save humanity in any way God chooses, God's decision to become human reveals the depth of God's goodness and love for fallen humanity. Jesus is the divine

1. Augustine, *Answer to Faustus* 20.11.

Word who became human to heal our wounded human nature and to share his divine life with us.

In *The Confessions*, Augustine admits that before he was instructed in the Catholic faith and baptized into the church, he had regarded Jesus simply as a wise teacher who provided humanity with a great example of practical discipline and spiritual guidance.[2] This view of Jesus was not uncommon in Augustine's time, nor is it uncommon today. However, as Augustine continued to study Scripture and the Christian tradition, he began to understand the importance of Christ as the mediator between God and humanity. Only by being both God and a human being could Christ provide the healing necessary for salvation and the gift of eternal life.

In a treatise against the Manichean bishop Faustus, Augustine affirmed that Christ is the one mediator as both God and man, for "in accord with the apostolic teaching, we said that Christ is not only God, so that we might put our hope in him with complete security, but also the mediator between God and men, the man Jesus Christ."[3] Christ is the "God-man, that is, in the Son of God, the savior, Jesus Christ, the mediator between God and men."[4] As the Son of God, Jesus is equal to the Father and the "form of God," and as a human being, Jesus takes on a fully human nature in the "form of a servant."[5] Some people mistakenly believe that Christ is only a man, and some believe that he is only God but not a human being. Christianity, however, declares that Christ is both God and human, and as such, Christ is the way to God.

The problem with Manichean Christology is the rejection of both Christ's divinity and humanity. According to the Manicheans, if God became a human, it would contaminate the divine nature. They argue Jesus could not have been born of Mary because human flesh has evil origins. Furthermore, Jesus is not fully God but merely a wise teacher who has come to share saving knowledge about the world's condition as a mixture of light and darkness.

2. Augustine, *Confessions* 7.19.25.

3. Augustine, *Answer to Faustus* 13.8.

4. Augustine, *Answer to Faustus* 13.8.

5. Augustine, *Answer to Faustus* 13.8.

Augustine refutes the flawed teachings of Manicheism by citing key scriptural verses such as 1 Tim 2:5, which states that Jesus Christ is the mediator between God and humanity. Similarly, Rom 8:5 emphasizes that Christ is above all things.[6] Christ is unlike any other creature since he is God, yet he is like all human beings because he was truly born of a woman.[7]

Paul's theology of Christ as the eternal Word made flesh and "born of a woman" (Gal 4:4) provided Augustine with an incarnational framework for his understanding of the relationship between visible and invisible, spiritual and material. In contrast to the Manicheans, Augustine did not view material bodily existence as an obstacle to God. Instead, the obstacle to God is sin. Christ is always holy and has a perfectly human nature without sin; yet he assumes human flesh and is sent by the Father to forgive our sins.[8]

The fact that Christ was truly born of a woman is essential to Christian teaching, for it demonstrates Christ's full humanity. "Our Lord and Savior Jesus Christ is the head of his body. He, the one mediator between God and humanity, the human Jesus, was born of a virgin in a solitary place, as we learn from the Book of Revelation. I think this mention of solitude is a way of saying that he alone was born of a virgin."[9] Christ alone is both God and human. By becoming a human being, the Word of God became flesh without changing flesh, that is, without changing human nature, while uniting humanity to God. "So, since the Word and God was a long way away from flesh and man, the Word became flesh, and joined man to God. . . . He taught us how to live, so that we might not die forever; he taught us how to die, so that we might live forever."[10] Christ is not only a wise teacher, but he is the one mediator who makes it possible for us to live forever by being united to God.

6. Augustine, *Answer to Faustus* 16.15.

7. Augustine, *Answer to Faustus* 16.15.

8. Augustine, *Answer to Faustus* 16.15.

9. Augustine, *Exposition of Psalm* 142.3.

10. Augustine, *Sermon* 313E.1.

As the mediator between God and humanity, Christ fulfilled the will of the Father and possessed a unique and saving grace. "In terms of the Son's divinity, the Father and the Son have one and the same will . . . he was not only man, but God and man . . . human nature could exist in him without any sin."[11] Since Christ did not have sin but had a perfect human nature, he could offer healing to fallen humanity.

CHRIST THE HEALER

Augustine's view of the human condition, as we experience it, is inevitably shaped by the effects of sin. We must remember that we live in a fallen world. The results of sin are evident in our daily lives. We encounter brokenness and alienation in our relationships with God, creation, and others. Human nature, although originally created good by God, is deeply affected by the fall of our first parents. We exist in an imperfect, corrupted state. We do not enter the world as blank slates, in moral neutrality. Instead, we are born into a condition where we lack the original communion and harmony that God intended. Due to our pride, we carry a wounded human nature. We are in need of deep healing and renewal. This healing can come only through the one mediator between God and humanity—Christ, the God-man.

According to Augustine, while we are on journey in this world, human beings are "beaten back" from our "home country" because of the "contrary winds of crooked habits" and by holding onto things "that are inferior and secondary" to what is "better and more worthwhile," namely, God.[12] All of humanity is in a state of sickness due to sin, a sickness revealed by the disordered love of material things above God. Nevertheless, God did not disdain the material world; instead, God chose to assume the human nature he created. In doing so, God provides the way for us to return to God. As he writes in *Teaching Christianity*, Augustine states that

11. Augustine, *Answer to Arian Sermon* 7.6.

12. Augustine, *Teaching Christianity* 1.9.9.

Christ, the Word and Wisdom of God, became flesh to heal our ills,[13] becoming the "way" to God by "deliberately making himself the pavement under our feet along which we could return home."[14] Since Christ has assumed the very human nature weakened or vitiated by sin, he is able to heal our disordered affections and restore what has been corrupted. This is possible only because he is both God and human, the divine source of life and truly a human being. Christ offers the medicine to heal our wounded nature. "The Son of God then assumed a human nature and bore patiently therein all human misery. The healing power of this medicine is beyond all comprehension. For what pride can be cured, if it is not cured by the humility of the Son of God?"[15] The humility of Christ is a balm that heals the sickness of our pride,[16] for since man had fallen through pride, Christ "applied humility to his cure."[17] Christ is the medicine who restores what has been lost and cures what has been corrupted, precisely as the Son of God who "revealed himself to us as a pattern of life."[18] Christ is the perfect model or example of humanity, and as the divine Wisdom, he makes the transcendent God accessible to spiritual creatures.[19]

Christ's full humanity is necessary in order to mediate divine life to us. "He could not have been a mediator had he not been human, because as God he is equal to the Father. . . . Christ is the mediator between humanity and God, not because he is God but because he is man."[20] Since Christ is both God and human, he is able to remake what he has made. This does not mean that Christ creates a new humanity, but rather that he restores and redeems what he made. "But the grace of God sets [human nature] free through faith in the one mediator of God and human beings, the man Jesus Christ, who, since he was God, made man and, while

13. Augustine, *Teaching Christianity* 1.10.10—1.14.13.

14. Augustine, *Teaching Christianity* 1.17.16.

15. Augustine, *Christian Combat* 11.12.

16. Augustine, *Sermon* 340A.1, 5.

17. Augustine, *Teaching Christianity* 1.14.13.

18. Augustine, *Christian Combat* 11.12.

19. Augustine, *Letter* 11.2–4.

20. Augustine, *Exposition of Psalm* 103[4].8.

remaining God and having become man, himself remade what he made."[21] Christ perfects and restores human nature without destroying his original creation.

In his mature teaching on Christ, Augustine clearly states that Christ had a fully human nature, body and soul, to heal our entire human nature.

> We know, and we hold firmly to the truth, that the mediator between God and men, the man Christ Jesus, insofar as he was man, was of exactly the same nature as we ourselves are. I mean our flesh and his flesh are not of different natures, nor our soul and his soul of different natures. He took on precisely that nature which he judged to be in need of saving. . . . And just as you, one human being, are soul and flesh, so too he, one Christ, is God and man.[22]

Christ's humanity is perfect, and therefore, it serves as the way to the godhead. That is, Christ's divine humanity acts as the mediating link to God. "Godhead without humanity doesn't mediate, humanity without godhead doesn't mediate. But what mediates between godhead in itself and humanity in itself is the human godhead and divine humanity of Christ."[23] Christ is the way to God through his perfect humanity, which is united to his divinity. Since he is God and human, he is both the way and the goal or the end of the journey. "For it is as man that he is the mediator, and it is as man, too, that he is the way: the goal as God, the way as man."[24] Christ is both the way to God for fallen humanity and the ultimate goal of humanity because he is God.

If we follow the way of Christ, we can receive the healing of our fallen human nature from the incarnate Word of God, who became human to reconcile us to God and to give us eternal life. For "when sins had separated the human race far from God, it was necessary for us to be reconciled to God for the resurrection of our

21. Augustine, *Letter* 177.11.
22. Augustine, *Sermon* 174.2.
23. Augustine, *Sermon* 47.21.
24. Augustine, *City of God* 11.2.

flesh to eternal life by the mediator who alone was born, lived and was killed without sin, so that human pride might be rebuked and healed by the humility of God."[25] Christ's humility heals our pride and reconciles us to God. "For he became the mediator for the purpose of reconciling us through humility to God, from whom we had through pride withdrawn a great distance."[26] The incarnation opens up to us the way to our heavenly home, for "he became man to reconcile to God those who were far off, to unite those who were divided, to recall the estranged and to bring back those sojourning away from home."[27] Christ directs those who are lost on the journey back to their heavenly homeland.

THE GRACE OF CHRIST

The grace of Christ the mediator not only forgives sins and reconciles us to God but also grants us a share in immortality. Augustine asserts in *The Confessions*, "In your unfathomable mercy you first gave the humble certain pointers to the true mediator. . . . This mediator between God and humankind, the man Christ Jesus, appeared to stand between mortal sinners and the God who is immortal and just: like us he was mortal, but like God he was just."[28] The grace of Christ acts as a remedy for wounded souls. "Grace is a medicine; if you want to be sick all the time, it means you are ungrateful for the medicine."[29] Christ is the great physician, whose grace can heal us. According to Augustine, this grace should be given even to infants because all human beings experience the effects of sin, namely, death. Since all die in Adam, all are given new life in Christ. "*Just as in Adam all die, so too in Christ shall all be made alive* (1 Cor 15:22). The only way [humanity] found of entering into the life of this world was through Adam; the only way it

25. Augustine, *Enchiridion* 28.108.
26. Augustine, *Letter* 140.28.68.
27. Augustine, *Exposition of Psalm* 100.3.
28. Augustine, *Confessions* 10.43.68
29. Augustine, *Sermon* 156.5.

will find of avoiding the penalties of the next is through Christ."[30] Christ is the new Adam, whose grace heals our wounded nature and offers us a share in everlasting life.

In Augustine's view, the incarnation was the most suitable or fitting way for God to save humanity, for it demonstrated the love of the mediator who came to cure us with his grace and to exalt us to the dignity of divine life.

> And it is not enough to rebut them by maintaining that this way God chose of setting us free through the mediator between God and men the man Christ *Jesus* (1 Tim 2:5) is good and befitting the divine dignity . . . there neither was nor should have been a more suitable way of curing our unhappy state. Nothing was more needed for raising our hopes and delivering the minds of mortals, disheartened by the very condition of mortality, from despairing of immortality, than a demonstration of how much value God put on us and how much he loved us.[31]

The incarnation reveals the depth of God's love, and Christ's redeeming work makes us children of God by the gift of the Holy Spirit. "So our reconciliation with God by a mediator and our reception of the Holy Spirit to make us children of the one to whom we were enemies—for all who are led by the Spirit of God are children of God (Rom 8:14): this is the grace of God through our Lord Jesus Christ."[32] Christ is the Word of God through whom all things were created, and his grace re-creates our fallen human nature. "He is our head, he who is God, equal to the Father, the Word through whom all things were made; but though as God he is our creator, he became man to re-create us. He is God to make us, but man to make us anew."[33] Christ became a human being in order to give us divine life. "You were human and could not reach God; God became human so that you, a human being who could reach another human but could not reach God, might attain to

30. Augustine, *Sermon* 293.11.

31. Augustine, *Trinity* 13.10.13.

32. Augustine, *Enchiridion* 10.33.

33. Augustine, *Exposition of Psalm* 90[2].1.

God through a man; and thus the man, Christ Jesus, became the mediator between God and humanity."[34] The grace of Christ not only heals our human nature but also elevates it so that we can share in divine life.

The grace of Christ is the source of our salvation, and Christ also serves as the perfect model or exemplar of humanity. For Christ enjoys a unique grace as the divine Word of God, yet he shares the same human nature with all human beings. "As regards that man, taken up by the Word, it's all grace, it's unique grace, it's perfect grace. . . . He took to himself a soul, he took to himself a body, he took to himself a complete human being."[35] Christ's human nature is exactly like ours, except without sin. "The mediator between God and men, the man Christ Jesus, insofar as he was man, was of exactly the same nature as we ourselves are. . . . He had nothing less than we do as regards nature, but he also had nothing by way of fault."[36] Christ possesses our human nature, yet since his nature is also divine, his humanity is perfectly graced. "Since he is the only God, by nature and not by grace, he became also the Son of Man that he might be full of grace as well."[37] Christ became human so that grace might be made available to fallen humanity. This is the grace of God that forgives sins and justifies sinners. "That great grace which is God's alone is here plainly shown, that men may understand that they are both freed from their sins and justified by the very grace which made Christ the man unable to have any sin."[38] As the mediator, Christ is the source of grace and salvation, and in his perfect humanity, he is the model for all of us on the journey to God.[39]

34. Augustine, *Exposition of Psalm* 134.5.

35. Augustine, *Sermon* 67.7.

36. Augustine, *Sermon* 174.2.

37. Augustine, *Enchiridion* 10.35.

38. Augustine, *Enchiridion* 11.36.

39. Since God's plan for perfecting humanity in Christ is accomplished in Christ, he also serves as the model of predestination: "There is also the most brilliant beacon of predestination and of grace, the savior himself, the very mediator between God and human beings, the man Jesus Christ" (Augustine, *Predestination of the Saints* 15.30).

Furthermore, in Augustine's developing Christology, the humanity of Christ becomes an instrument of his divinity. That is, Christ's graced humanity serves as the instrument by which God heals and elevates our human nature. For the unity of the divine and human natures in Christ has made grace, in a way, natural to him so that Christ might redeem humanity.

> The manner in which Christ was born of the Holy Spirit not as a son and of the virgin Mary as a son shows us the grace of God by which a man without any preceding merits, at the very beginning of his natural existence, was joined to the Word of God in so great a personal unity that the Son of God was Son of Man and the Son of Man Son of God, and thus in the assumption of human nature grace itself, which cannot allow any sin, became in some way natural to that man.[40]

Christ's perfect humanity is essential to his salvific work because it is the means by which God's grace operates. Christ offered himself as a sacrifice for sins to reconcile humanity to God (2 Cor 5:20–21). By participating in Christ's incarnation, death, and resurrection—the paschal mystery—human beings can die to their sins and share in new life.[41] This participation in Christ's salvific work is mediated by the sacraments of the church, particularly baptism. "This is the great mystery of baptism which is celebrated among us, that all who share in that grace may die to sin, just as he is said to have died to sin because he died to the flesh, that is, to the likeness of sin, and that they might have life by being reborn from the font, whatever their physical age, just as he had life when he rose from the grave."[42] The mystery of baptism makes possible our participation in the grace of Christ and in his passing over from death to eternal life. Christ's unique grace as the mediator between God and humanity is mediated through the sacraments, especially baptism and the Eucharist.[43] The sacraments incorporate new

40. Augustine, *Enchiridion* 12.40.

41. Augustine, *Enchiridion* 13.41.

42. Augustine, *Enchiridion* 13.42.

43. Augustine, *Homilies on Gospel of John* 26.19.

members into the one body of Christ, who together with Christ, the head, form the whole Christ (*totus Christus*). The idea of the whole Christ is a central feature of Augustine's mature Christology.

THE WHOLE CHRIST

As Augustine explains in one of his sermons, Christ can be understood in three ways: (1) God, the eternal Word who is equal to the Father; (2) the God-man, the mediator between God and humanity; and (3) the whole Christ, that is, Christ the head and the members of his body, the church. This understanding of Christ emerges from the Scriptures.

> Our Lord Jesus Christ, brothers and sisters, as far as I have been able to tune my mind to the sacred writings, can be understood and named in three ways. . . . The first way is: as God and according to the divine nature which is coequal and coeternal with the Father before he assumed flesh. The next way is: when, after assuming flesh, he is now understood from our reading to be God who is at the same time man, and man who is at the same time God, according to that pre-eminence which is peculiar to him and in which he is not to be equated with other human beings, but is the mediator and the head of the church. The third way is: in some manner or other as the whole Christ in the fullness of the church, that is as head and body, according to the completeness of a certain *perfect man* (Eph 4:13), the man in whom we are each of us members.[44]

The whole Christ is formed by the building up of the church as Christ's body. For we know Christ as our mediator and savior, but the mystery of God's saving plan is to invite human beings to become members of his body, the church. "We know him thus as the whole Christ, which means Christ in this universal sense, Christ with his church. But He alone was born of the Virgin, and He alone is the church's head, He who is the mediator between

44. Augustine, *Sermon* 341.1.

God and humankind, Christ Jesus."[45] Christ the head was born of Mary as evidence of his true humanity. Now human beings can be joined to Christ's humanity in order to become one body. "But if he is the head, and we are the body, the whole Christ consists of head and body."[46] In Augustine's view, Scripture points to the mystery of the whole Christ. The Psalms, for instance, speak about Christ the head or the members of his body, the church. "Be ready for Christ to speak to us, Christ who is both head and body. We must always, or nearly always, hear Christ's voice speaking from a psalm in such a way that when we contemplate our head, the one mediator between God and humankind, himself human, Christ Jesus, we do not contemplate him in isolation."[47] The figures of Scripture are signs that point to the mystery of the whole Christ.

In Augustine's interpretation of the Old Testament, the patriarchs and prophets who preceded Christ in time are, nevertheless, members of the body of Christ. They believed in Christ insofar as they were faithful to God. Christ was hidden among them, yet they had faith in God, and so they had faith in Christ. "How could the patriarchs have failed to know him or to believe in him, when they deserved the name of prophets because they proclaimed the Lord in advance, even though in a hidden way? They must have believed in him, because no one is reconciled with God, whether before the incarnation or after it, except through the faith that is in Christ Jesus."[48] Augustine teaches that the righteous people of the Old Testament had faith in Christ because they had faith in God's saving work, which would be accomplished by the incarnation. "Whoever were able to be righteous among the people of the Old Testament were also set free only through the same faith by which we too are set free, that is, faith in the incarnation of Christ, which was foretold to them as it was announced to us now that it has taken place."[49] Those who came before Christ are saved

45. Augustine, *Exposition of Psalm* 90[2].1.
46. Augustine, *Exposition of Psalm* 58[1].2.
47. Augustine, *Exposition of Psalm* 58[1].2.
48. Augustine, *Exposition of Psalm* 104.10.
49. Augustine, *Letter* 157.3.14.

because they believed that God would send a Savior. "By the most salutary faith in Christ, who is both God and man, those righteous people were also saved who, before he came in the flesh, believed that he would come in the flesh."[50] All the righteous are members of Christ's body, whether before or after the incarnation.

Another key feature of Augustine's view of the whole Christ is that the righteous are spread throughout the world and across time. "He became the head of the church, and so he has a body and limbs. Look for his limbs. At present they are groaning throughout the whole world, but at the end they will be full of joy over that crown of righteousness."[51] Just as Christ's body has been present on earth before the head, so it will be perfected at the end of time. "The church has been present on earth since the dawn of humanity; holy Abel was its first-fruits, Abel, who was slain in witness to the blood that would be shed one day by the mediator, put to death in his turn by a faithless brother."[52] The Catholic Church is the universal church, spread throughout the world. "It is the Church that he just called his only one; this is the only Catholic one which, is spread abundantly through the whole world, which, by growing, stretches out to the most distant nations."[53] The church has existed since Abel and will continue until Christ's return. Until that time, the church mediates grace as the body of Christ. The church's sacraments bring about new members of Christ's body. Baptism is the sacrament of regeneration, by which new members are incorporated into the one body. In Augustine's time, this included the practice of baptizing both adults and infants. "Nothing else is accomplished by the baptism of little ones but that they are incorporated into the church, that is, that they are joined to the body and members of Christ."[54] Baptism gives birth to charity in the members, that is, to the twofold love of God and neighbor that

50. Augustine, *Letter* 190.1.6.

51. Augustine, *Exposition of Psalm* 100.3.

52. Augustine, *Exposition of Psalm* 118[29].9.

53. Augustine, *Letter* 140.17.43.

54. Augustine, *Punishment and Forgiveness* 3.4.7.

unites the one body.[55] The church is formed as one body by the invincible "knot of unity and love."[56]

Augustine interprets the figures of the Old Testament as foreshadowing the formation of the whole Christ. Adam and Eve symbolize Christ and the church because, just as Eve was created from Adam's side, the church is also born from Christ's side through the sacraments, represented by the blood and water that flowed from his side on the cross.[57] The church is the body and bride of Christ, without stain or wrinkle (Eph 5:27), yet she must undergo a process of growth and transformation to be purified from sin. She is the chaste spouse and virgin mother because of her teachings from Christ; however, she is also filled with sinners in need of grace. The church is the temple of God, composed of true and genuine Christians, but during this time, it is a mixed body of saints and sinners, the good and the wicked. The church contains both wheat and chaff, for the weeds are found among the wheat (Matt 13:24–30) until God separates them at the end of time. Until then, there is an intermingling of the good and wicked within the church.

Likewise, Noah's ark symbolizes the church on its journey through history. The entrance to the ark is baptism, which is the sacrament of forgiveness of sins.[58] During its earthly journey, the church consists of both good and wicked, represented by the pairs of animals on the ark. Yet in the end, God will separate the saints from the sinners. Some who partake in the sacraments will be cast out in the end, while others who are outside the visible body will be united with the church's communion in charity at some future point in time.[59] This does not mean there is a separate communion of believers outside the church; rather, there is only one communion in charity, mediated by the visible church, to which all members of Christ's body will be united.

55. Augustine, *Teaching Christianity* 2.6.7.

56. Augustine, *Teaching Christianity* 1.16.15.

57. Augustine, *On Genesis* 2.24.37; *Homilies on Gospel of John* 9.10.

58. Augustine, *Answer to Faustus* 12.16.

59. Augustine, *Answer to Faustus* 12.20, 12.22.

In Augustine's view, there is only one body of Christ, whose soul is the Holy Spirit.[60] The Holy Spirit unites the different members of the one body by the fiery bonds of charity.[61] All of the just, beginning with Abel, are members of the one body because the power of the sacraments extends beyond the limits of time and space. The Holy Spirit mediates charity through the visible church's rituals, but the Spirit cannot be limited by them. Those catechumens who were martyred before baptism received baptism by blood.[62] All who are brought into the church's unity in charity must love unity in order to share in the charity enjoyed by the saints. "He who does not love the church's unity does not have God's charity, and for that reason it is rightly understood to be said that the Holy Spirit is not received except in the Catholic Church."[63] The visible church is the ordinary means of salvation and incorporation into the one body of Christ.

As his view of the church as the one body of Christ continued to develop, Augustine singled out Peter as a leader among the apostles. Peter, identified as the rock by Christ in Matt 16:19, is a sign of the unity of the whole Christ, head and members. Peter is a symbol of the church as the way of salvation. The bishops are successors of the apostles, and apostolic succession is a safeguard of the church's unity in doctrine, practice, and charity. "If, after all, we must consider the order of bishops in succession, how much more certainly and in a way truly conducive to salvation would we begin from Peter himself, who symbolized the whole church."[64] The church finds unity around the successor of Peter, the bishop of Rome, for Peter is a sign of the whole church. In the end, the true body of Christ will be constituted by the good, "whether those who are already spiritual or those who by their peaceful obedience are making progress toward spiritual things. It is not in the bad, though, whether they are acting troublesomely outside [the

60. Augustine, *Sermon* 267.4; 268.2.

61. Augustine, *Answer to Faustus* 12.24.

62. Augustine, *Baptism* 4.17.24.

63. Augustine, *Baptism* 3.16.21.

64. Augustine, *Letter* 53.2.

church] or are being endured with groaning within, both baptizing and being baptized."[65] The invisible bonds of unity and peace are maintained by those members bound together by charity who form the one body of Christ.

THE CHURCH IN TRANSFORMATION

Augustine's nuanced understanding of the church as the body of Christ is significant for all of us on our journey to God. As we have seen, Augustine teaches that the church on earth is a mixed body of saints and sinners, undergoing transformation until her final purification at the end of time. Only God knows those whom he predestined before the foundation of the world (Rom 8:29). There are many outside of the church who might be joined to the one body and bride of Christ without stain or wrinkle.[66] The number of the righteous will be revealed on the last day, but until then, the good and the wicked are mixed together in the church, such that "many who seem to be outside are within, and many who seem to be within are outside."[67] According to Augustine, Christians should not be surprised to encounter scandal within the church, as there will always be sinners among the members. At the same time, the church should never lose hope for those outside its boundaries, for there are some who will be joined to the church at a future time.

Augustine's understanding of the church's mixed condition is meant to give hope to the church on journey. For God foreknew those who would fall away, yet God also willed that some would be saved or predestined according to his plan. The doctrine of predestination is not the same as a pagan view of fate or determinism, but it is about God's will to confer grace upon human beings to build up the heavenly kingdom. "But God willed that so many be created and born who he foreknew would not pertain to his grace that they outnumber by an incomparable amount those whom he

65. Augustine, *Baptism* 3.18.23.

66. Augustine, *Baptism* 4.3.4.

67. Augustine, *Baptism* 5.27.38.

graciously predestined to be children of the promise for the glory of his kingdom."[68] Uncertainty about one's salvation need not lead to despair; instead, it should be a reason for hope. While a believer's inner disposition must stay open to charity, in Augustine's teaching, charity is a gift freely given to the faithful by the Holy Spirit through grace. The ordinary means of grace are the sacraments, which are effective and holy regardless of the condition of the minister or recipient. If someone commits a serious sin, they can receive forgiveness by undergoing reconciliation and performing penance under the guidance of the local bishop.[69] This makes it possible for the members of the church to undergo a process of growth and transformation, such that the members of the body are more and more conformed to Christ, the head. The spiritual life is a gradual yet steady progression and growth in sanctification through participation in the church's sacramental and communal life.

The church's goal is to be conformed to Christ, the head, by growing in the virtues of faith, hope, and charity. Growth in virtue is a sign of progress on the way to our heavenly homeland, where Christ reigns.

> Our head, Christ, is already in heaven, but our enemies can still rage against us. . . . He said that he was here below in us; therefore we are also there above in him, because even now he has raised my head above my enemies. Look how wonderful a pledge we have, assuring us that we too are in heaven for ever with our head, in faith and hope and love, because our head is with us on earth in divinity, in goodness, in unity, even to the consummation of this age.[70]

By the virtues of faith, hope, and charity, the members of the church already begin to share in the life of heaven with the head, while Christ takes on the sufferings of the members on journey.

68. Augustine, *Letter* 190.3.12.

69. The local bishop could assign the appropriate forms of penance, which might last several years.

70. Augustine, *Exposition of Psalm* 26[2].11.

"Without him, we are nothing, but in him we too are Christ. Why? Because the whole Christ consists of head and body. The head is he who is the savior of his body, he who has already ascended into heaven; but the body is the church, toiling on earth."[71] Those who come after Christ and are incorporated into the church are members of Christ's body.

Augustine presents a rich theology of suffering, in which the members of Christ's body on earth undergo transformation by suffering in union with the head in heaven. The members suffer while they are on the journey, but their sufferings can be joined to Christ, the head. Christ does not suffer in heaven, but he grants the members of his body a share in his heavenly glory while he takes on their suffering.

> And that's why the same apostle, while he was still Saul, heard the words, *Saul, Saul, why are you persecuting me?* (Acts 9:4); because the body is joined to the head. And when as a preacher of Christ he was now suffering from others what he had done himself as a persecutor, *that I may fill up*, he said, *in my flesh what is lacking from the afflictions of Christ* (Col 1:24); thus showing that what he was suffering was part and parcel of the afflictions of Christ. This can't be understood of the head, which now in heaven is not suffering any such thing; but of the body, that is the church; the body, which with its head is the one Christ.[72]

The members of the church, as members of Christ's body who have been incorporated by baptism, can say that they are Christ, while following Christ the head to the heavenly homeland. "Having put on Christ we, with our head, are Christ."[73] The church is the city of God on journey in this world, whose hope is fixed in heaven. "This city originates from Abel, as the wicked city derives from Cain. This city of God is therefore very ancient. Tolerating the

71. Augustine, *Exposition of Psalm* 30[2].3.

72. Augustine, *Sermon* 341.1.

73. Augustine, *Exposition of Psalm* 100.3.

earth, its hope is fixed on heaven."[74] By uniting their suffering with Christ the head, the members of Christ's body grow in faith, hope, and charity, and they make progress on the way to their heavenly homeland. Together with the saints and angels, the members of the church on earth form the one city of God. The image of the church as city provides deeper insight into Augustine's understanding of spiritual transformation while on the journey to heaven.

THE CITY OF GOD

According to Augustine, the church is the city of God on journey to her final heavenly destiny. Christ is the king of the heavenly city, and he is the way to God. "The king himself came down and made himself the way for us on our pilgrimage, so that by walking in him we may not go astray, or faint on the journey, or fall in with robbers, or stumble into the traps that are set alongside the path."[75] Christ is the one true king and priest foretold in the Hebrew Scriptures. God gave Christ the throne promised to David so that there might be no end to his kingdom as the one mediator between God and humanity.[76]

Christ the mediator suffered and died to redeem the members of the heavenly city on journey, which "is composed of human beings like ourselves. It has been redeemed from all sin by the blood of the mediator who has no sin."[77] The angels rejoice at the redemption accomplished by Christ, for the "holy angels, taught by God . . . know how large a number of members of the human race is required to complete that city."[78] Augustine speculates that the number of redeemed human beings will make up for the number of fallen angels, such that "by the redemption of men the

74. Augustine, *Exposition of Psalm* 142.3.
75. Augustine, *Exposition of Psalm* 90[2].1.
76. Augustine, *Agreement Among the Evangelists* 1.3.6.
77. Augustine, *Enchiridion* 16.61.
78. Augustine, *Enchiridion* 16.62.

losses caused by the fall of the angels are made good."[79] Christ's death reconciles heaven and earth, and it brings about the perfect completion of the heavenly city of God. The church remains on pilgrimage until every citizen of the heavenly city is created and brought into communion with the one body of Christ.

The citizens of the two cities, Jerusalem and Babylon, are intermingled during the present age, but the citizens of the wicked city can become members of the heavenly city by receiving baptism. The heavenly city is built up by the incorporation of new members into the church. While on journey, the good must bear with the wicked in order to be conformed to the patience and forbearance of God that leads to repentance.[80] The final winnowing will take place when the grain and straw are separated by God, so that the faithful drawn from the human race are joined with the heavenly angels to form the one city and temple of God. "So this church, which exists among the holy angels and powers of God, will be known to us as it is when we are joined with it at the end to share in unending blessedness."[81] The church is on journey toward its final union with the entire city of God in heavenly glory.

In anticipation of the final union of the whole Christ at the end of time, the church's liturgical celebration signifies and makes present the unity of the one body of Christ on earth and in heaven. The church's celebration of the Eucharist is a participation in the fellowship of the saints and angels in heaven.

> Thus by this food and drink he wishes that the fellowship of his body and of his members be grasped; that fellowship is the holy church in his saints and his faithful, who have been predestined, and called, and justified, and glorified. . . . The sacrament of this reality, that is, of the unity of Christ's body and blood, is placed on the Lord's table and received from the Lord's table—in some places every day, in others at fixed intervals of time, leading

79. Augustine, *Enchiridion* 16.61.

80. Augustine, *Instructing Beginners in Faith* 25.48.

81. Augustine, *Enchiridion* 16.61.

> some to life and others to ruin. But, the reality itself, of which this is the sacrament, means life for all.[82]

The sacrament of the Eucharist celebrated at the Lord's altar unites the "whole redeemed city, that is, the congregation and fellowship of the saints," as one body and one sacrifice.[83] This is the true religion found in the worship of Christians, wherein the whole city of God is united as a living sacrifice. The church's role is to offer the true sacrifice of the whole Christ, head and members, at the eucharistic altar as a body of charity and a means of grace for the transformation of the earthly city into the heavenly city. As we shall see, participation in the church's sacramental life is essential to Augustine's vision of the spiritual life.

CONCLUSION

In this chapter, we have examined Augustine's understanding of Christ as the way to God. What is at stake in our journey is nothing less than human salvation. For Augustine, salvation involves healing our wounded human nature and participating in the divine life. Our humanity can be healed only through Christ, the God-man, who took on human nature to heal it. By receiving Christ's grace, we can share in his divinity. God's grace becomes accessible through the church, which is the body of Christ. As Augustine emphasizes, all members of the church need healing because of the sickness of sin. Augustine asserts that such healing can happen only by means of grace, which is mediated by the church's sacraments. Together with Christ the head, the church forms the whole Christ. The members of Christ's body on earth undergo transformation by growth in faith, hope, and charity, especially amid suffering. The next chapter explores the spiritual life as a healing process that occurs within a community offering liturgical worship and acts of reconciliation, all aimed at becoming the one body of Christ united in love.

82. Augustine, *Homilies on Gospel of John* 26.15.

83. Augustine, *City of God* 10.6.

4

The Ongoing Journey

Life in the Spirit

And just as your body, if it is without spirit, which is your soul, is dead, so too your soul, if it is without the Holy Spirit, that is without charity, will be counted as being dead.

—Augustine, *Homilies on the Gospel of John* 9.8

SINCE WE LIVE IN a fallen world, how can we make progress on our journey to God? What are some practical ways to grow in our spiritual lives? As members of the church, what does it mean to be transformed and conformed to Christ, the head? Augustine offers practical wisdom in response to these questions. Although he is often remembered for his lofty theological and philosophical teachings, it is important to remember that Augustine was first and foremost a pastor. He excelled at making the mysteries of the Christian faith accessible, practical, and relevant to everyday life for his congregation. For Augustine, Christianity is not a spectator sport. Instead, it requires the members of the church to live according to divinely revealed teachings and to grow in virtue. Christian doctrine and practice are closely intertwined. As a spiritual leader, Augustine understood this, and he provided practical guidance for spiritual growth.

In this chapter, we will explore Augustine's practical wisdom for Christian living. According to Augustine, spiritual growth requires developing virtue. Specifically, he emphasizes the virtues of faith, hope, and charity, which are unique because they rely on God's grace. These virtues are facilitated by the sacraments of the church and are deepened by our cooperation with God's grace. By receiving the sacraments, we continue to advance on the spiritual journey and become more conformed to Christ as members of his one body, united in love through the Holy Spirit.

It is also important to remember that, in Augustine's view, our spiritual transformation can happen only within community. We are social beings, and we do not exist in isolation from others. Salvation is always communal because we are saved as members of the one body of Christ. While we can develop personal devotions and spiritual practices, we must always remember that our growth takes place as members of the communal body of Christ—that is, the church. Finally, we will explore Augustine's insights into the practice of prayer. As a bishop and spiritual leader, Augustine was often asked about how to pray, and he offers timeless wisdom for those seeking to deepen their prayer life. At the same time, Augustine never separates personal piety from charitable works. That is, performing good works is vital to the spiritual life because, in Augustine's view, the church is one body united in charity. By offering charitable works, we strengthen our union with Christ, the head, and his body, the church.

THE LIFE OF VIRTUE

Augustine defines virtues as good habits that enable us to grow toward perfection. Above all, the virtues are gifts given by God, yet we can choose to cooperate with God's grace as children of God. "Yes, we to be sure can say that it is by our virtues, by our good habits, by our style of life that we have earned the right to be made into children of God."[1] The greatest virtues are the theological

1. Augustine, *Sermon* 174.2.

virtues, as they are traditionally called—faith, hope, and charity. Faith is what makes one righteous, as a gift of God's grace.[2] Hope is a specific virtue for the church on journey toward its heavenly homeland. Charity is the greatest theological virtue, for charity perfects all of the virtues. Virtue is measured by growth in charity. "Now, as for love, which the apostle says is greater than the other two, that is faith and hope, the greater it is in a person, the better is that person in whom it is."[3] Love is the greatest virtue because it leads us to eternal life. "For although he cannot hope without love, it may be that he does not love that without which he cannot reach that for which he hopes, for instance if he hoped for eternal life—and who does not love that?"[4] Charity is the greatest of the commandments, and the end of all of them. "So all the divine commandments concern charity, of which the apostle says: *The end of the commandment is charity that comes from a pure heart, a good conscience, and sincere faith* (1 Tim 1:5). Thus charity is the end of every commandment, that is, every commandment concerns charity."[5] The entire life of virtue is concerned with charity.

Since our ultimate goal is union with God in love, charity is the aim and goal of our spiritual journey. Faith works through love, and all virtues are ordered toward love. "Because faith cannot work well, except through love . . . the faith to be admired, the true faith of grace, is the sort that works through love."[6] The Holy Spirit gives the church the gift of love, for God is love.

> Now to have love, and to be able to have good works as a result of it, is that something we can give ourselves, seeing that it is written, *The love of God has been poured out in our hearts through the Holy Spirit which has been given to us* (Rom 5:5)? So entirely is love or charity the gift of God that it is even called God, as the apostle John says:

2. Augustine, *Letter* 177.11.
3. Augustine, *Enchiridion* 31.117.
4. Augustine, *Enchiridion* 31.117.
5. Augustine, *Enchiridion* 32.121.
6. Augustine, *Sermon* 156.5.

> *Charity is God*, and whoever remains in charity remains in God, and God in him (1 Jn 4:16).[7]

Charity is a gift given to the church to provide healing, specifically through the sacraments. Augustine uses the parable of the good Samaritan to illustrate the healing that takes place within the church (Luke 10:25–37). The man left "lying in the road half-dead by robbers" is the whole human race, that is, humanity in its fallen, wounded condition. Christ is the good Samaritan who passes by and has mercy on us.[8] Christ binds our wounds with wine and oil, which are symbols of the sacraments of baptism and the Eucharist. He takes the man to the inn, which is the church.[9] Finally, he gives two denarii to the innkeeper, signifying twofold charity, that is, the love of God and the love of neighbor.[10] We are healed by growth in charity as part of the community of the church.

Augustine's view of transformation in charity promotes a compassionate, gentle pastoral approach rather than a harsh one, as it allows for growth while trusting in God's mercy given through the sacraments. Instead of relying solely on one's personal efforts to grow in faith, hope, and charity, one can trust in the gradual work of grace administered by the sacraments and reflected in the life of the community. Additionally, Augustine's emphasis on human weakness fosters greater understanding and compassion toward others. In this view, one is not surprised by human sinfulness, nor does one vilify the sinner. At the same time, one does not ignore shortcomings but encourages growth and healing through participation in a sacramental community. This fosters true charity as the foundation for the unity of the church.

According to Augustine, charity is not a human invention but instead finds its source in the Holy Spirit (Rom 5:5). The church can withstand any scandal among its members and preserve its unity because of the presence and work of the Spirit, who brings

7. Augustine, *Sermon* 156.5.

8. Augustine, *Exposition of Psalm* 30[2].8.

9. Augustine, *Sermon* 179A.7; *Sermon* 131.6; *Questions on the Gospels* 2.19.

10. Augustine, *Exposition of Psalm* 125.15.

together a diverse group of people with a heavenly unity from above.[11] The charity of the Holy Spirit is the glue that binds the members of the church together. No matter their condition, there is always room for growth, transformation, and healing because the Spirit is constantly at work.

The grace of Christ is a healing balm that helps overcome pride, which is a kind of addiction. Pride, or *superbia*, is healed by the humility found in the Word, which is sweeter than anything else.[12] The healing that comes from Christ is fostered by frequent participation in the sacraments. Augustine understood baptism to be the beginning of a lifelong process of convalescence rather than an instantaneous cure.[13] Baptism marks the beginning of the spiritual path of salvation for Christians, who undergo healing and transformation by sharing in the sacramental life of the church.

THE SACRAMENTAL LIFE

In Augustine's view, the sacraments are essential for growth in the spiritual life. These religious rituals were established by Christ and were prefigured by ancient Jewish traditions. The rites of the Old Testament were signs pointing to the sacraments given by Christ. "For those former sacraments were promises of things that were to be fulfilled, but these sacraments are proofs of their fulfillment!"[14] For Augustine, baptism is essential for salvation since baptism incorporates one into the body of Christ and offers the grace of the mediator. "I am certain that there is absolutely no soul in the human race that does not need for its deliverance the mediator between God and human beings, the man Jesus Christ (1 Tim 2:5)."[15] The grace of Christ is mediated by means of the sacraments, and

11. Augustine, *Answer to Faustus* 12.16.

12. Cavadini, *Visioning Augustine*, 23–44.

13. Markus, *End of Ancient Christianity*, 54.

14. Augustine, *Answer to Faustus* 19.14.

15. Augustine, *Letter* 166.2.5.

Augustine emphasizes the need for participation in a visible, communal body celebrating the sacraments to grow in charity.

Along with baptism, the Eucharist is a special sacrament that builds up the church. Like baptism, the efficacy of the sacrament originates from Christ. When celebrated by a validly ordained minister, the bread and wine are transformed into the body and blood of Christ. For Augustine, the Eucharist signifies not only the flesh and blood of Christ but also the unity of the whole Christ, comprising both head and members, as one body in charity. Sharing in eucharistic fellowship also means building up a community modeled on the early church. The life of the community in Jerusalem described in Acts 2:43–47 serves as the primary example of the Christian community in anticipation of the heavenly life of the blessed. The ideal of sharing possessions and goods among the local congregation is to be emulated by all. By loving one's neighbors, one is loving Christ. Augustine did not limit almsgiving to members of the church, for Christians should be generous to all. The church's union in charity through the Eucharist necessarily overflows with works of mercy.

Furthermore, the Eucharist is the sacrament of God's mercy, for it mediates the mercy of Christ, the mediator between God and humanity. This mercy is the essence of sacrifice, as prefigured by the sacrifices of the old law in the Old Testament. "And thus, through the unique sacrifice in which the mediator was immolated, which the many sacrifices of the Old Law prefigured, things in heaven are reconciled with things on earth, and things on earth with things in heaven."[16] Christ's sacrifice is the true and perfect sacrifice, and this "great mercy" (*magnam misericordiam*) purifies humanity from sin and causes us to cling to God as our final end.[17]

Augustine links Christ's supreme sacrifice with the "daily sacrifice of Christians" offered at the eucharistic altar. "At the same time, he is also the priest, himself making the offering as well as himself being the offering. And he wanted the sacrifice offered by the church to be a daily sacrament of his sacrifice, in which the

16. Augustine, *Enchiridion* 16.62.

17. Augustine, *City of God* 10.20.

church, since it is the body of which he is the head, learns to offer its very self through him."[18] The supreme offering of Christians includes the whole Christ, head and members, united in charity. The church offers works of mercy in union with Christ's perfect work of mercy on the cross.

By offering true worship, the members are transformed and configured to the head (Rom 12:2), such that the whole city "is offered to God as a universal sacrifice through the great priest who, in his passion, offered himself for us in the form of a servant, to the end that we might be the body of such a great head."[19] Any true work of mercy is a sacrifice insofar as it leads one and one's neighbor to be united to God in charity. For "true sacrifices are works of mercy, whether shown to ourselves or shown to our neighbors, which are directed to God."[20] The perfect work of mercy offered by Christ on the cross infuses all of the church's works of mercy, and these good works can be united to the one sacrifice of Christ offered at the eucharistic altar. In Augustine's view, the true and supreme sacrifice consists of the offering of the whole Christ (*totus Christus*) united as a living body of mercy, offered at the eucharistic altar as a sacrifice of mercy. This is the sacrifice that "the church continually celebrates in the sacrament of the altar (which is well known to the faithful), where it is made plain to her that, in the offering she makes, she herself is offered."[21] The church offers herself at the eucharistic altar as a living body of mercy, in union with Christ's saving sacrifice on the cross. This is the sacrifice that is pleasing to God, namely, the sacrifice of the whole Christ.

The eucharistic life of the church means receiving the mercy of God and being conformed to that mercy while offering works of mercy to one's neighbors, such that the members of the church become living "vessels of mercy."[22] The Eucharist is the sacrament of mercy that not only nourishes the members of Christ's body but

18. Augustine, *City of God* 10.20.

19. Augustine, *City of God* 10.6.

20. Augustine, *City of God* 10.6.

21. Augustine, *City of God* 10.6.

22. Augustine, *City of God* 21.24.

also sends the members out into the world to offer works of mercy in union with the mercy of Christ the head. Augustine presents a dynamic view of Christian worship that inevitably yields works of mercy among the members of the one body of Christ.

The sacramental life enables human beings to progress on their journey to God by becoming detached from worldly things and clinging to God. Through baptism, the church gives birth to spiritual persons, who no longer cling to the things of this world, but rather cling to God in love.[23] Baptism gives birth to charity in the members, while reception of the Eucharist deepens the virtues of faith, hope, and charity. This is due to the power of Christ, who instituted the sacraments as sources of grace.[24] Spiritual persons are incorporated into the living body of charity. This includes all of the just persons before and after Christ's incarnation. The sacraments are the normal means of grace for the members of the church, but God is not limited by them.

In Augustine's time, church membership was a lifelong process of purification and growth in holiness in order to be saved. Christian parents often enrolled their children as catechumens shortly after they were born, but many delayed baptism. There was no clear minimum length of the catechumenate for adult converts, and many who were dedicated as infants lived as catechumenates for most of their lives. They regularly attended sermons, especially from the bishop, but were not allowed to be present for the eucharistic prayer and communion. Baptism could be celebrated at any time, but Easter was the most appropriate time. At the beginning of the Lenten preparation each year, catechumens would be invited to submit their names for baptism, and they would be baptized during the Saturday Easter Vigil service. They were clothed in white linen, symbolizing purity and new birth, before being anointed with oil and receiving the imposition of hands calling down the Holy Spirit. This conferred a sharing in Christ's universal priesthood, and the newly baptized were expected to join the community for prayer, eucharistic communion, and works of mercy.

23. Augustine, *Baptism* 1.15.23.

24. Augustine, *Answer to Faustus* 19.13–14.

Then, after being incorporated into the body of Christ, the members of the church were sent out to proclaim the gospel and to offer works of mercy as members of Christ's body.

THE SACRAMENT OF RECONCILIATION

Among the common practices of the Christian community in North Africa was the practice of reconciliation, which was necessary after post-baptismal sin. During Augustine's time, reconciliation required confession in public or private, the performance of penitential works, and formal release from guilt. Among the serious sins were murder, adultery, and fornication. Other sins included theft, robbery, false witness, as well as the list provided by Paul in Gal 5:19–21, including sorcery, enmity, jealousy, anger, dissension, party spirit, envy, and drunkenness. Common sins of daily living included the immoderate use of bodily necessities, failures in social interactions, and lapses of attention during prayer. These sins of daily living could be forgiven by private and communal recitation of the Lord's Prayer, and by almsgiving and fasting. Serious sins, however, required reconciliation according to the penitential practices determined by the local bishop. Those guilty of serious sin were required to abstain from the Eucharist.

Augustine argued that all sins could be forgiven by means of the ritual of reconciliation. Charity covered a multitude of sins, both major and minor. Serious sins required formal public penance as determined by the bishop. The length of penance was established by the bishop according to the particular sin. The clergy were the ministers of reconciliation, but the power to forgive sins was received from the Holy Spirit as the gift of charity possessed among the society of saints, that is, all those united in love. Like baptism, the sacrament was efficacious through the ritual, but the interior disposition of the penitent was also significant, for the penitent had to have the intention of union with the saints. Since the Holy Spirit is the source of the unity and holiness of the church, the Spirit's gift of charity unites the members as one body. This communion of charity could forgive serious sins due to the divine power given to the saints. The only unforgivable sin against the Holy Spirit was a rejection of the church's unity and a failure to seek forgiveness.[25] According to Augustine, the bishops were not responsible for the efficacy of the sacrament themselves, even though they determined proper penitential practice and served as the ministers of reconciliation. The Holy Spirit belongs to all of the saints, not merely to the bishops and clergy.

The clergy received the laying on of hands to serve as valid ministers to the flock. As shepherds of Christ's flock, bishops had to bear the burden of rendering to God an account of their stewardship. The clergy follow the example of Christ, the good shepherd, whose voice the sheep will follow. The pastor must learn to strengthen the feeble sheep (Ezek 34:4), not by offering a false hope nor by breaking them with terror. Instead, the pastor must remind them that God is faithful and that God will not allow one to be tempted beyond what one can bear (1 Cor 10:13). The pastor cannot promise absolute well-being in this world, but the shepherd can promise God's constant mercy. This is the source of true hope for the church, as it enables the sheep to bear trials and temptations along the way. By encouraging the sheep in this way, the pastor strengthens the weak and provides a bandage of consolation for the wounded. By administering the sacraments, the minister offers the mercy and compassion of Christ, who suffers with his sheep and feeds them with his healing love. Just as pastoral ministry is a source of Christ's love, so too Christian matrimony is a source of Christ's grace for the church on earth.

THE SACRAMENT OF MARRIAGE

According to Augustine, marriage is a sacrament that fosters healing in the context of a domestic community. In his treatise *The Excellence of Marriage*, Augustine understands marriage prior to the coming of Christ as a sign and sacrament that prefigured the

25. Augustine, *Sermon* 71.23.37.

subjection of all people to God.[26] Marriage is a symbol that the church will be united to Christ definitively in the one heavenly city. After Christ's incarnation, marriage is a sign that makes present the healing and transformative love of Christ for the church in anticipation of the final unity of the city of God. Augustine has a strikingly positive view of the goodness of marriage.

Augustine identifies three primary goods of marriage: (1) procreation; (2) fidelity of the spouses; and (3) sacrament, which has a broad definition.[27] Marriage in the Old Testament was established by God as a prophetic sign of Christ and the church. After the coming of Christ, as in the New Testament and the early church, marriage is sacrament insofar as it makes present Christ's love for his bride, the church. In two treatises composed around the year 401, entitled *The Excellence of Marriage* and *Holy Virginity*, Augustine sought to defend celibacy without denigrating the goodness of marriage. For Christians, marriage is a sacrament of unity, for "out of many souls there will arise a city of people with a single soul and single heart turned to God," and "this perfection of our unity will come after this pilgrimage, when no longer will anyone's thoughts be hidden from another, and no longer will anyone be in conflict with anyone about anything."[28] Although perfection of unity will be realized only in heaven, even now, Christian marriage is a sign and instrument of the unity of the whole body of Christ. This means that marriage as a sacrament mediates the mystery of Christ's spousal love for the church, which has the effect of binding together the members of the church as one body.

In Augustine's view, a subsequent but no less important feature of Christian marriage as a sacrament follows, namely, indissolubility. The value of marriage for all people lies in the objectives of procreation and the faithful observance of chastity or mutual fidelity, but for the people of God, marriage is elevated because of the sanctity of the sacrament, which has the consequence of

26. Augustine, *Excellence of Marriage* 18.21.

27. Augustine, *Excellence of Marriage* 24.32.

28. Augustine, *Excellence of Marriage* 18.21.

indissolubility until the death of husband or wife.[29] The emphasis upon indissolubility is evident in later works against the Pelagians, such as the treatise *Marriage and Desire.* In this work, Augustine points to the marriage of Joseph and Mary, which realized all three goods—offspring, fidelity, and sacrament—since the offspring is "the Lord Jesus, fidelity because there was no adultery, and the sacrament because there was no divorce."[30] While Joseph and Mary are a unique case, all three goods are present in their marriage, just as all three must be present in the sacrament of Christian marriage, for Augustine declares, "That which is something great, then, in Christ and the church is quite small in each individual husband and wife, but it is still a sacrament of an inseparable union."[31] Marriage is indissoluble because it is a sign of the inseparable union between Christ and his bride, the church.

In his work *Literal Meaning of Genesis,* Augustine considers how marriage between a man and a woman is a sign of the union of the whole human race. Prior to the fall, Augustine argues that Adam and Eve would have enjoyed sex and procreation without any experience of lust.[32] However, after their disobedience and rejection of God, human beings no longer enjoy the original union and communion of paradise, a state sometimes called original justice. As a result, human beings are born into a condition of corruption and separation from God, from others, and between soul and body. Yet as Augustine makes clear, sex itself is not evil, for it is a good created by God. The problem is not sexuality; the problem is sin and the effect of sin, that is, concupiscence. Augustine asserts that Christian marriage can put a bad thing to a good use. In this case, marriage puts to use the concupiscence of the flesh, whose

29. Augustine, *Excellence of Marriage* 24.32.

30. Augustine, *Marriage and Desire* 1.11.13.

31. Augustine, *Marriage and Desire* 1.21.23.

32. In his *Answer to Pelagians,* Augustine maintains his argument that the first human beings in paradise would have had intercourse "as often as they desired, or they would have held desire in check when intercourse was not necessary. . . . Or without any passion present there at all, the sex organs would have in their proper activity obeyed without any difficulty the commands of the will, just as the other members do for their respective activities" (1.17.34).

effects cannot be eradicated entirely during this life, for the good of procreation.[33] For Augustine, sexuality remains good even if the persons are in a weakened or vitiated state due to original sin.

> We do not, however, find fault with bread and wine because of those who eat and drink too much, just as we do not find fault with gold because of those who are greedy and miserly. For the same reason we do not find fault with the proper union of spouses because of the shameful passion of bodies. For that union of spouses could have existed, even if no sin had first been committed, and the couple would not have been ashamed over it. But this passion came to be after the sin, and in their shame they were forced to conceal it. As a result of this, though their married descendants make good and licit use of this evil, they avoid being seen by other human beings when engaged in this act, and in that way they admit that it is a source of shame, since no one ought to be ashamed of what is good.[34]

The sacrament of marriage puts to good use the evil of concupiscence, which is experienced by married persons most keenly in conjugal union. The conjugal union of spouses can be an act of charity and mercy despite the effects of concupiscence.[35] Augustine is clear that concupiscence is not itself a sin in those who have been baptized,[36] for it is a particular sort of bad quality, like a disease,[37] or as a kind of vitiation, corruption, or absence of an intended good, just as a disease is an absence of health. We can be redeemed only by the grace of Christ, mediated by the sacraments of the church. Augustine's teaching on the sacramentality of marriage affirms the goodness of human nature, while at the same time insisting upon the need for God's grace. Human nature is inherently good and worthy of saving, for "if human nature were

33. Augustine, *Punishment and Forgiveness* 1.29.57.

34. Augustine, *Marriage and Desire* 2.21.36.

35. Augustine, *Sermon* 354A.7.

36. Augustine, *Marriage and Desire* 1.22.24.

37. Augustine, *Marriage and Desire* 1.25.28.

something evil, it ought not to be saved, and if there were nothing evil in it, it would not need to be saved . . . we should not accuse marriages because of the evil which the merciful savior must heal in them."[38] Christ alone was conceived without concupiscence or sin so that he could save and heal human nature,[39] while all who are conceived after the fall are born into concupiscence and are in need of a savior. Marriage as a sacrament mediates the healing grace of Christ among the spouses.

Because of concupiscence, marriage is a struggle against the effects of sin.[40] Marriage demonstrates the ongoing struggle against original sin and the need for Christ, the divine physician.[41] However, marriage remains a good because it is a sacred sign that points to the unity of the human race fulfilled in Christ and the church, which was prefigured by marriage in the Old Testament. After Christ's coming, marriage is an instrument of Christ's spousal love. Marriage as a sacrament mediates Christ's spousal love and unites the spouses as one body, signifying the union of the whole church. For Augustine, the Christian family, which arises from marriage, can be likened to the church as a domestic church. According to God's plan, marriage and family provide the natural context in which the members of the church learn to grow in charity, that is, the twofold love of God and neighbor, which offers healing and union. For married Christians, healing is a gradual process that includes hope for the redemption of the body, for although we remain under the effects of sin, the body "still has hope of redemption, because in eternal beatitude nothing at all of sinful concupiscence will remain . . . after it has been healed of that plague and disease and has been completely clothed with immortality."[42] All Christians can look forward to the resurrection from the dead, wherein our bodies will no longer be subject to corruption and decay but instead will share in the glory of immortality.

38. Augustine, *Marriage and Desire* 2.21.26.

39. Augustine, *Marriage and Desire* 1.12.13.

40. Augustine, *Answer to Julian* 3.16.30.

41. Augustine, *Marriage and Desire* 2.29.50.

42. Augustine, *Marriage and Desire* 1.31.35.

In Augustine's view, Christian marriage and the practice of celibacy for the kingdom are complementary because they are signs that point to heavenly immortality.[43] Celibacy and matrimony are distinct states of life, but all Christians are called to be vigilant in other common practices, such as prayer, liturgical worship, and works of mercy. Individuals offer these practices within a larger community, namely, the church. The spiritual life, therefore, is best understood in the context of communal growth and transformation. Prayer in particular is essential to progress on the spiritual journey. For Augustine, prayer is both private and public, and it is inherently linked to almsgiving. Growth in love for God naturally leads to growth in love for others. An Augustinian spirituality leads to a deeper love of God, self, and neighbor, and it is marked by a commitment to a life of prayer and almsgiving.

PRAYER AND ALMSGIVING

According to Augustine, prayer is a movement of the heart that fosters love for God above all things, yet this love draws us to love God's creatures, including ourselves and our neighbors, as God loves them. Augustine notes that the great commandment to love your neighbor as yourself (Mark 13:21) means loving three things: (1) God, (2) oneself, and (3) one's neighbor. "Two commandments given: love God and love your neighbor, and yet I see three things to be loved. After all, it wouldn't say *and your neighbor as yourself*, unless you were also to love yourself."[44] To love ourselves and our neighbors means to love God as our final end, and to bring our neighbors to share in this same love. "In him we, of course, love ourselves if we love God, and by the other commandment we truly in that way love our neighbors as ourselves if we bring them, to the extent we can, to a similar love of God. We, therefore, love God on account of himself and love ourselves and our neighbors on

43. Augustine, *Holy Virginity* 11.13.

44. Augustine, *Sermon* 179A.4.

account of him."[45] By loving God, we are led to God as our final end, and we have truly loved ourselves. Now we are able to love our neighbors as ourselves, namely, to God as end. "So this is your love, or love of yourself, that is, the love you love yourself with: to love God. Now I can also entrust your neighbor to you, whom you are to love as yourself."[46] God's love leads us to love ourselves and our neighbors as God's beloved creatures.

Prayer directs us to love God as our final end and happiness. Yet God is to be enjoyed not in isolation but in community. "And the supreme reward is that we should enjoy [God] and that all of us who enjoy him should also enjoy one another in him."[47] Liturgical worship draws the community of the church into the proper worship of God. True community is found in the love of God, for God makes it possible for us to love God and to love one another. For Augustine, to love properly means to recognize that God is the beginning and the aim of all loving. To love God with the whole of ourselves is to love ourselves truly, and to love our neighbors as ourselves means to bring them to share in the enjoyment of God.

The life of prayer is grounded in the church's communal participation in the sacraments. However, Augustine also instructs Christians on how to advance in private prayer, which inevitably leads to practices such as almsgiving. According to Augustine, prayer is an exercise of the heart's desire for God, which can be continuous. "This very desire is your prayer, and if your desire is continuous, your prayer is continuous too."[48] Although the desire for God is continuous, Augustine recommends setting aside certain times for prayer, including in the morning and evening.[49] Following the example of Christ, Augustine advocates the repetition of the Lord's Prayer, for it is a reminder that Christ prays "in us as our head, and he is prayed to by us as our God."[50] Prayer is

45. Augustine, *Letter* 130.7.14.

46. Augustine, *Sermon* 179A.4.

47. Augustine, *Teaching Christianity* 1.32.35.

48. Augustine, *Exposition of Psalm* 37.14.

49. Augustine, *Letter* 130.9.18.

50. Augustine, *Exposition of Psalm* 85.1.

not a solitary endeavor, for prayer is a means of union between Christ, the head, and the members of his body, the church. Prayer expands our hearts so that they can be filled with God himself.[51] God knows what we want before we ask him, yet prayer teaches us how to desire God with our whole heart.[52] Thus, prayer enables us to practice loving God above all things, so that we can cling to God in love. Furthermore, prayer inevitably leads to almsgiving, for prayer is an exercise of true charity. As such, insofar as the heart is purified, it can rightly direct its loves to God and neighbor.

Prayer disposes the heart to love properly. When Christ teaches us to pray in our bedrooms (Matt 6:6), this means the bedrooms of our hearts, where God comes to dwell.[53] Only by loving God above all things can one love oneself and one's neighbor properly, that is, by loving them to God. Almsgiving, therefore, must be directed toward the greatest good of one's neighbor, which is to cling to God.[54] Works of mercy are most effective when they are offered for God's sake, that is, to bring all to share in God's love. Prayer enables us to grow in true charity, which is the love of God, oneself, and one's neighbor in the proper order.

While prayer and the sacraments make it possible to grow in charity while on our earthly journey, the final enjoyment of God with others is reserved for heaven. In our heavenly homeland, we will share in the eternal happiness of praising God with our neighbors and with all of creation forever. In the meantime, we can begin to praise God in this life by practicing works of mercy and engaging in the church's sacramental life. Growth in the spiritual life means an increase in virtue, especially faith, hope, and charity. As we advance in these virtues, we make progress toward our final end, which is to praise God without ceasing in heaven.

51. Augustine, *Homilies on First Epistle of John* 4.6.

52. Augustine, *Letter* 130.8.17; *Lord's Sermon on the Mount* 2.3.14.

53. Augustine, *Lord's Sermon on the Mount* 2.3.11.

54. Augustine, *Lord's Sermon on the Mount* 2.2.9.

CONCLUSION

Augustine's understanding of the spiritual life is grounded in his view of the Holy Spirit as charity, the very charity that binds together the members of the church. Without charity, there is no life in the body of Christ. For just as the Holy Spirit is the love that proceeds from the Father and the Son, so too the Holy Spirit pours forth charity in order to unite the members of Christ's body.[55] As the soul of the one body of Christ, the Holy Spirit gathers together people from all over the world to share in the eternal divine life of love.

The spiritual life, in Augustine's view, cannot be lived out apart from an embodied community united in love. While the work of the Holy Spirit is invisible, nevertheless, the Spirit works primarily in the midst of a visible, communal body that celebrates the sacraments and engages in Christian practices, including liturgical worship, private prayer, and almsgiving. An Augustinian spirituality is a lifelong process of transformation, in which our hope is placed in the healing that occurs by participation in the sacraments, especially baptism, the Eucharist, and reconciliation. For some, Christian marriage is a sacrament that mediates the spousal love of Christ for the church. For others, celibacy serves as a sign of heavenly immortality. For all members of the church, prayer and almsgiving lead to an increase in charity, which yields progress on our journey to our heavenly homeland. Despite the effects of our fallen condition, we can undergo true healing by receiving the grace of the sacraments and by participating in the communal life of the sacraments. Our hope lies in the slow but transformative healing offered by Christ, the divine physician, and the work of the Holy Spirit to form the one body of Christ united in love.

55. Augustine, *Trinity* 6.5.7.

Conclusion

Praise Without Ceasing

Live good lives, and you yourselves will be his praise.
—Augustine, *Sermon* 34.6

ACCORDING TO AUGUSTINE, GROWTH in the spiritual life is a gradual process of transformation and conformation to Christ through faith, hope, and charity. It involves healing from pride or *superbia*, which is the disordered desire to take the place of God. This healing can happen only through the grace of Christ. By receiving God's grace, our loves can be reordered so that we can learn to cling to him above all things and then love ourselves and our neighbors properly. Our restless heart reveals to us that we are created for a transcendent end. Only God fulfills the deepest desire of our heart. We are on a journey to our heavenly homeland, where our heart will find rest. Until then, we make progress on the journey by participating in the sacraments and by engaging in Christian practices, such as prayer and almsgiving, which foster growth in virtue—especially the virtue of charity. In this life, we are travelers seeking our true heavenly homeland. But God has not abandoned us; he has shown us how to make this journey through Christ and the church. By receiving the grace of the sacraments, we learn how to cling to God as members of the one body of Christ united in love.

For Augustine, the life of true blessedness is a life dedicated to praising God. In Augustine's view, praise is the antidote to pride, because by praising God, we learn how to forget ourselves. If we praise God as our greatest good, then we can truly love ourselves and our neighbors. The happy life, then, is a life of praise and gratitude to God, who is the source of our being and the end of our longing.

Augustine's spirituality is defined by learning how to praise God in this life so that we can praise him for eternity. As Augustine declares in *The Confessions*, praise is a confession of God's mercy. "Accept the sacrifice of my confessions . . . allow my soul to give you glory that it may love you the more, and let it confess to you your own merciful dealings, that it may give you glory. Your whole creation never wearies of praising you."[1] To become praise means to become a witness of God's healing and merciful love. By receiving God's mercy in his word and sacraments, one can begin to experience deep healing from the sickness of sin. With the help of grace, one learns to give thanks and praise for God's loving mercy and compassion. And by living a life of praise and thanksgiving in conformity to Christ, one can learn to love one's neighbor while clinging to the infinite mercy and compassion of the God who became our neighbor.

For Augustine, the spiritual life is a eucharistic life of thanksgiving and praise. The Eucharist is the sacrament of "mercy," through which individuals receive God's mercy and are shaped by it, while also offering acts of mercy to others. The members of the church become living vessels of mercy, praising God for his merciful work within them. This testimony can transform hearts and minds and draw those who have distanced themselves from God into the church as a living body of mercy. The ultimate goal of the eucharistic life is to say thank you to God for his mercy and to invite others to join in this act of gratitude and praise.

During our earthly journey as members of Christ's body, we become God's praise by living good lives in conformation to Christ, the head. "Do you want to sing God his praises? Be yourselves what you sing. You are his praise if you lead good lives."[2]

1. Augustine, *Confessions* 5.1.1.

2. Augustine, *Sermon* 34.6.

The virtues God gives us to live good lives will lead us to the true happiness of eternal life. "By these virtues given by God through the grace of Jesus Christ . . . we now live a good life, and afterwards we will be given its reward, the happy life, which can only be eternal life."[3] By growing in virtue, we make progress on the road to eternal life. "We are only going to receive the happy, blessed life, when we come to him who came to us, and when we begin to be with him who died for us."[4] Our ultimate happiness is realized in the next life, where corruption and despair no longer exist. Until then, we find joy in the hope of eternal praise.

> There, there is praising and being happy and joy. Afterward, then, not now, is there any happiness. Where is it now? It's in hope. You don't yet hold it in your hand, but you can rejoice by hoping, because the one who promised it cannot disappoint, because the one who promised it has it and gives it.[5]

In our heavenly homeland, both soul and body will give praise to God for eternity. "This faith of ours, however, promises on the strength of divine authority, not of human argument, that the whole man, who consists of course of soul and body too, is going to be immortal, and therefore truly happy."[6] The martyrs provide us with an example of living faith, for they offered their lives as sacrifices of praise to the living God. We ought to follow in their footsteps, so that together we may give praise as friends of God. "Our happiness redounds to his praise, because it is he that turns us from being miserable into being happy creatures."[7] God alone makes us happy, and our eternal happiness gives him praise.

In the end, the saints give praise to God, for they reveal God's mercy. By loving God, the saints become the goodness that they love. "It is to our advantage to love him whom we praise because,

3. Augustine, *Letter* 155.4.16.
4. Augustine, *Sermon* 231.5.
5. Augustine, *Sermon* 45.10.
6. Augustine, *Trinity* 13.9.12.
7. Augustine, *Sermon* 335H.2.

by loving the good, we become better."[8] God does not wait for us to do good in order to be loved, but rather by loving us, God makes us good. "Knowing that it is good for us to love him, God has made himself lovable by praising himself. . . . He therefore stirs up our hearts to praise him, and he has filled his servants with his own Spirit, to enable them to offer him praise."[9] By loving the good which is God, we find our greatest good and we become part of the eternal praise of heaven.

God's greatness is manifested by his love for free creatures who come to love him freely. They learn to love what he commands and praise him freely, without any coercion. This gives greater glory and praise to God. "Consequently, a human being would not have the desire for the good from the Lord, if it were not good, but if it is good, we have it from no one but from him who is supremely and immutably good."[10] Human beings cannot do any good apart from God; nevertheless, they must choose to love and to obey him freely.

God is the source of love by which we love and do the good, such that God's commands become sweet to us. The life of praise, therefore, becomes sweet to us in this life so that we can continue to praise God for eternal life. "If love is from God, we have the whole of it from God. . . . And so, the blessing of sweetness is the grace of God by which he brings it about in us that we find delight in and we desire, that is, that we love what he commands us."[11] God's commandments become sweet to us because they bring us to delight in God during this life, in anticipation of the life to come.

The praise of God that begins on earth will continue in heaven. In Augustine's vision, this will be our eternal activity. "What will our occupation be? To praise God, to love him and praise him, to praise him out of love, and to love him as we praise."[12] We must learn to praise God in this life to prepare for our eternal life of

8. Augustine, *Exposition of Psalm* 144.1.

9. Augustine, *Exposition of Psalm* 144.1.

10. Augustine, *Answer to Pelagians* 2.9.21.

11. Augustine, *Answer to Pelagians* 2.9.21.

12. Augustine, *Exposition of Psalm* 147.3.

praise. "Our thoughts in this present life ought to be centered on the praise of God, because to praise God will be our everlasting joy in the life to come, and no one will be fit for that future life unless he or she is well practiced in the art of praising God now."[13] The works of mercy here will be superseded there, and together we will find our rest in God. Yet this rest does not mean inactivity. For our activity in heaven will be praise without ceasing. "This will be our activity: praising God. If you love him, you also praise him."[14] The final destination of our spiritual journey is to praise God forever. "*They will praise you for ever and ever.* This will be the work that occupies us totally, an 'Alleluia' that never fades away."[15]

13. Augustine, *Exposition of Psalm* 148.1.

14. Augustine, *Exposition of Psalm* 85.24.

15. Augustine, *Exposition of Psalm* 83.8.

Bibliography

Augustine. *Agreement Among the Evangelists.* Translated by Kim Paffenroth. In WSA I/15.

———. *Answer to an Arian Sermon.* Translated by Roland J. Teske. In WSA I/18.

———. *Answer to an Enemy of the Law and Prophets.* Translated by Roland J. Teske. In WSA I/18.

———. *Answer to Faustus, a Manichean.* Translated by Roland J. Teske. WSA I/20.

———. *Answer to Julian.* Translated by Roland J. Teske. In WSA I/24.

———. *Answer to Secundus, a Manichean.* Translated by Roland J. Teske. In WSA I/19.

———. *Answer to the Two Letters of the Pelagians.* Translated by Roland J. Teske. In WSA I/24.

———. *Baptism.* Translated by Maureen Tilley and Boniface Ramsey. In WSA I/21.

———. *The Catholic Way of Life and the Manichean Way of Life.* Translated by Roland J. Teske. In WSA I/19.

———. *The Christian Combat.* Translated by Robert Russell. In FC 2. Washington, DC: Catholic University of America Press, 1950.

———. *The City of God.* Translated by William Babcock. 2 vols. WSA I/6–7.

———. *The Confessions.* Translated by Maria Boulding. WSA I/1.

———. *Continence.* Translated by Ray Kearney. In WSA I/9.

———. *Enchiridion.* Translated by Bruce Harbert. In WSA I/8.

———. *The Excellence of Marriage.* Translated by Ray Kearney. In WSA I/9.

———. *Expositions of the Psalms.* Translated by Maria Boulding. 6 vols. WSA III/15–20.

———. *The Happy Life.* Translated by Ludwig Schopp. In FC 5. Washington, DC: Catholic University of America Press, 1948.

———. *Holy Virginity.* Translated by Ray Kearney. In WSA I/9.

———. *Homilies on the First Epistle of John.* Translated by Boniface Ramsey. WSA III/14.

———. *Homilies on the Gospel of John.* Translated by Edmund Hill. WSA III/12.

———. *Instructing Beginners in Faith*. Translated by Raymond Canning. WSA V.

———. *Letters*. Translated by Roland J. Teske. 4 vols. WSA II/1–4.

———. *The Literal Meaning of Genesis*. Translated by Edmund Hill. In WSA I/13.

———. *The Lord's Sermon on the Mount*. Translated by Michael G. Campbell. In WSA I/15.

———. *Marriage and Desire*. Translated by Roland J. Teske. In WSA I/24.

———. *The Nature and Origin of the Soul*. Translated by Roland J. Teske. In WSA I/23.

———. *On Genesis: A Refutation of the Manichees*. Translated by Edmund Hill. In WSA I/13.

———. *The Perfection of Human Righteousness*. Translated by Roland J. Teske. In WSA I/23.

———. *The Predestination of the Saints*. Translated by Roland J. Teske. In WSA I/26.

———. *The Punishment and Forgiveness of Sins and the Baptism of Little Ones*. Translated by Roland J. Teske. In WSA I/23.

———. *Questions on the Gospels*. Translated by Roland J. Teske. In WSA I/16.

———. *Sermons*. Translated by Edmund Hill. 11 vols. WSA III/1–11.

———. *The Spirit and the Letter*. Translated by Roland J. Teske. In WSA I/23.

———. *Teaching Christianity*. Translated by Edmund Hill. WSA I/11.

———. *The Trinity*. Translated by Edmund Hill. WSA I/5.

———. *True Religion*. Translated by Edmund Hill. In WSA I/8.

———. *Unfinished Work in Answer to Julian*. Translated by Roland J. Teske. In WSA I/25.

Babcock, William. "Augustine and the Spirituality of Desire." *Augustinian Studies* 25 (1994) 179–99.

Bullivant, Stephen. *Nonverts: The Making of Ex-Christian America*. New York: Oxford University Press, 2022.

Cavadini, John C. *Visioning Augustine*. Challenges in Contemporary Theology. Hoboken, NJ: Wiley, 2019.

Chadwick, Henry. *Augustine of Hippo: A Life*. New York: Oxford University Press, 2010.

Fuller, Robert C. *Spiritual, but Not Religious: Understanding Unchurched America*. New York: Oxford University Press, 2001.

Guardini, Romano. *The Conversion of Augustine*. Translated by Elinor Briefs. Westminster: Newman, 1960.

Irizar, Pablo, and Anthony Dupont. "Many as One: Augustine's Onefold Ecclesiology." *International Journal of Philosophy and Theology* 82 (2021) 1–16.

Le Fébure du Bus, Emmanuel-Marie. *Desire and Unity: Augustinian Spirituality for Today*. San Francisco: Ignatius, 2022.

Lee, James K. *Augustine and the Mystery of the Church*. Minneapolis: Fortress, 2017.

Levering, Matthew. *The Theology of Augustine: An Introductory Guide to His Most Important Works*. Grand Rapids: Baker Academic, 2013.

Markus, Robert. *The End of Ancient Christianity*. New York: Cambridge University Press, 1991.

Martin, Thomas F. *Our Restless Heart: The Augustinian Tradition*. Maryknoll, NY: Orbis, 2003.

Mattis, Jacqueline S. "Spirituality [Religiousness, Faith, Purpose]." In *Character Strengths and Virtues: A Handbook and Classification*, edited by Christopher Peterson and Martin E. P. Seligman. New York: Oxford University Press, 2004.

Possidius. *The Life of St. Augustine*. Translated by F. R. Hoare. Western Fathers. New York: Sheed and Ward, 1954.

Smith, Christian. *Souls in Transition: The Religious Life of Emerging Adults in America*. With Patricia Snell. New York: Oxford University Press, 2009.

Smith, James K. A. *On the Road with Saint Augustine: A Real-World Spirituality for Restless Hearts*. Grand Rapids: Brazos, 2019.

Teresa of Avila. *The Book of Her Life*. In *The Collected Works of St. Teresa of Avila*, translated by Kieran Kavanaugh and Otilio Rodriguez, vol. 1. Washington, DC: ICS, 1987.

Topping, Ryan N. S. *St Augustine*. Bloomsbury Library of Educational Thought. New York: Bloomsbury, 2010.

Weinberg, Steven. "The Cosmological Constant Problem." *Reviews of Modern Physics* 61 (1989) 1–23.

Name/Subject Index

Scripture Index

Works of Augustine

www.ingramcontent.com/pod-product-compliance
Lightning Source LLC
LaVergne TN
LVHW051005080826
845145LV00009B/2460